THE INDO-EUROPEANS:
IN SEARCH OF THE
HOMELAND

ALAIN DE BENOIST

THE INDO-EUROPEANS

IN SEARCH OF THE HOMELAND

TRANSLATED BY AARON CHEAK, PHD

LONDON
ARKTOS
2016

www.arktos.com

ISBN	978-1-910524-86-2 (Softcover)
	978-1-910524-87-9 (Hardback)
	978-1-910524-91-6 (E-book)
BIC-CLASSIFICATION	Indo-European Languages (2A)
	Prehistoric archaeology (HDDA)
	Historical and comparative linguistics (CFF)
EDITOR	John B Morgan
TRANSLATION	Aaron Cheak
COVER DESIGN	Andreas Nilsson
LAYOUT	Tor Westman

CONTENTS

A NOTE FROM THE EDITOR

U nless otherwise indicated, the footnotes to the text were added by the author himself in the original French edition. Additional footnotes which were added by me or the translator for this edition for clarification are marked with either an 'Ed.' or 'Tr'. Where sources in other languages have been cited, I have attempted to replace them with their equivalent English-language editions when they could be located. Citations to works for which I could locate no translation are retained in their original language.

JOHN B MORGAN
Budapest, Hungary
15 July 2016

TRANSLATOR'S PREFACE

Originally published in 1966 as *Les Indo-Européens* (GED), Alain de Benoist's text appeared in a revised and expanded edition in 1997 as *Indo-Européens: à la recherche du foyer d'origine* (Nouvelle École). The present translation derives from the text of the 1997 edition. The most literal translation of the title is *Indo-Europeans: In Search of the Original Homeland*. However, we have followed Benoist himself, who in the text gives 'homeland' (rather than 'original homeland') as the English equivalent of *foyer originel*. Cohering with standard use in Indo-European studies, the numerous appearances of *foyer d'origine* and *foyer original* (cf. German *Urheimat*) throughout the text have also been rendered as 'homeland' for concision and impact.

Throughout this work, Benoist references a wealth of scholarly literature from Indo-European studies and related disciplines, such as archaeology, anthropology, and comparative religions. In addition to French authors, he cites primarily from German and English scholarship. Very frequently, studies originally written in English appear in French translation when quoted in Benoist's text. In those cases where it was not possible to source Benoist's original citations in the original English, what is presented in this translation, therefore, is a faithful representation in English of the quotations as given in French in Benoist's text. Full citations are given by Benoist throughout for those who wish to follow up the original language references. Titles of works in foreign languages that appear in the main body of the work have been presented in their original languages, per Benoist's original text, and glossed in English for the convenience of the reader.

Aaron Cheak, PhD

THE INDO-EUROPEANS:
IN SEARCH OF THE HOMELAND

Although foreseen at the end of the sixteenth century, notably by Leibniz[1] and the Florentine Filippo Sassetti,[2] the kinship of the principal Indo-European (IE) languages[3] was formally established in the first half of the nineteenth century. However, one often considers that the celebrated communication presented on 2 February 1786 by Sir William Jones (1746–1794) before the Royal Asiatic Society of Calcutta, of which he was the founder, represents the launching point for IE studies. Employed as 'Chief Justice' of the British East India Company of Bombay, Jones, having successively learned Latin, Greek, Welsh, Gothic, and Sanskrit, gained the sense that these languages probably derived from a common ancestor. 'The *Sanscrit* language, whatever be its antiquity', he declared before the Royal Asiatic Society, 'is of a wonderful structure; more perfect than the *Greek*, more copious than the *Latin*, and more exquisitely refined than either, yet bearing to both of them a

---

1 Gottfried Wilhelm Leibniz (1646–1716) was a highly influential German mathematician and philosopher. — Ed.

2 Filippo Sassetti (1540–1588) was a Florentine traveler who travelled to Goa, India in 1583 and remained there for the rest of his life, and was one of the first Europeans to study Sanskrit, which led him to discover correspondences between it and Italian, which presaged the later discovery of the Indo-European language group. — Ed.

3 The words 'Indo-European' and 'Indo-Europeans' are here systematically abbreviated as 'IE'. They are conserved integrally only in the titles of books or articles, as well as in quotes. We have also adopted the abbreviation 'PIE' to designate 'Proto-Indo-European' or 'Proto-Indo-Europeans' (that is, not the pre-Indo-European populations, but the IE in the stage immediately preceding their initial dispersion). Concerning the titles of publications, the name of the *Journal of Indo-European Studies*, published in Washington, has been abbreviated to '*JIES*'. For the transcription of diacritic signs, we have adopted the usual conventions. The sign for length is noted by two points (:). Recall that a word preceeded by an asterisk (*) is a word which is not attested historically, but results from a reconstruction.

stronger affinity, both in the roots of verbs and the forms of grammar, than could possibly have been produced by accident; so strong indeed, that no philologer could examine them all three, without believing them to have sprung from some common source, which, perhaps, no longer exists; there is a similar reason, though not quite so forcible, for supposing that both the *Gothic* and the *Celtic*, though blended with a very different idiom, had the same origin with the *Sanscrit*; and the old *Persian* might be added to the same family, if this were the place for discussing any question concerning the antiquities of Persia'.[4]

The ideas of Jones were popularised by Friedrich von Schlegel[5] (*Über die Sprache und Weisheit der Indier*, 1808),[6] before being reprised and deepened by the linguists Rasmus Rask (1787–1832) and Franz Bopp (1791–1867), who were the first to systematically compare the grammar of the different IE languages. Founder of Nordic philology, and precursor of modern general linguistics, Rask would publish the first scientific grammar of Icelandic in 1811; subsequently, in 1814, he wrote a monograph proving the kinship of this language with Slavic, Baltic, Greek, and Latin. Franz Bopp, trained in the study of Sanskrit by Antoine de Chézy, published a treatise on the conjugation system of Sanskrit in 1816. His great work, *Grammaire comparée du sanskrit, du zend, du grec, du latin, du lithuanien, du vieux slave, du gothique et de l'allemand*[7] appeared in five volumes from 1833 to 1852. His works were translated and popularised in France by Michel Bréal[8] (1832–1915).

---

4   'The Third Anniversary Discourse, on the Hindus', delivered to the Asiatic Society, 2 February 1786, in *Sir William Jones: Selected Poetical and Prose Works*, ed. Michael J Franklin (Cardiff: University of Wales Press, 1995), pp. 355–370.

5   Karl Wilhelm Friedrich von Schlegel (1772–1829) was a German poet and philosopher who is credited with being the intellectual founder of German Romanticism. — Ed.

6   Carl Wilhelm Friedrich von Schlegel, *On the Language and Wisdom of the Indians* (London: Ganesha, 2001). — Ed.

7   *A Comparative Grammar of the Sanskrit, Zend, Greek, Latin, Lithuanian, Gothic, German, and Sclavonic Languages*, 3 vols. (London: Williams & Norgate, 1882). — Ed.

8   Michel Bréal was one of the founders of the modern discipline of semantics. — Ed.

Shortly thereafter, while Kaspar Zeuss (*Die Deutschen und die Nachbarstämme*, 1837)[9] would explore the morphological correspondences between the Slavic and Germanic languages, Adalbert Kuhn (*Zur ältesten Geschichte der indogermanischen Völker*, 1845),[10] on the basis of a systematic comparison of the Indo-Aryan and Slavic languages, formulated the programme that would become 'linguistic palaeontology'. In 1852, Kuhn would also found the first journal of comparative grammar, the *Zeitschrift für vergleichende Sprachforschung*,[11] which would exercise a considerable influence, notably on Johann Wilhelm Mannhardt (1831–1880), director from 1885 of the *Zeitschrift für deutsche Mythologie und Sittenkunde*.[12] The first etymological dictionary of the IE languages was published in 1859 by August Friedrich Pott (*Etymologische Forschungen auf dem Gebiete der indogermanischen Sprachen*).[13] During the same period, the Anglo-German linguist Friedrich Max Müller (1823–1900),[14] who wrote a thesis on the comparative philology of the IE languages (and won the Volney Prize from the Institut de France in 1849),[15] laid the foundations for the comparative history of religions. Adolphe Pictet,[16] for his part, would systematically explore the vocabulary. All these efforts would lead to the formation of the 'Neogrammarians'[17] gathered around Karl

---

9   *The Germans and Neighbouring Tribes.* — Tr.

10 *On the Earliest History of the Indo-Germanic Peoples.* — Tr.

11 *Journal for Research in Comparative Linguistics.* — Tr.

12 *Journal for German Mythology and Customs.* — Tr.

13 *Etymological Researches in the Field of Indo-Germanic Languages.* — Tr.

14 Max Müller was a German who lived in England for most of his adult life. An important pioneer in the then-budding field of Indology and a student of Sanskrit, his studies and translations were groundbreaking for their time and continue to influence the field. — Ed.

15 The French Institute is an academic society consisting of five academies, which has been in existence since 1795. Alain de Benoist himself won the Grand Prize from the French Academy, one of its organs, in 1978 for his book *Vu de droite*. — Ed.

16 Adolphe Pictet (1799–1875) was a French linguist of the Romantic school who was an important figure in comparative linguistics. — Ed.

17 The Neogrammarians were a linguistic movement which originated in nineteenth-century Leipzig, that postulated that when changes in the sounds of a language oc-

Brugmann, whose monumental *Grundriß der vergleichenden Grammatik der indogermanischen Sprachen*[18] was published in Strasbourg from 1886.

IE studies, the further history of which will not be traced here, has continued to grow. It remains above all the purview of linguistics, but also appeals to archaeology, anthropology, comparative mythology, ancient history, the history of religions, sociolinguistics, and so forth.[19] On the archaeological map, the intensive excavations which have been undertaken since 1945, notably in Russia and in the Balkans, have allowed for better knowledge of prehistoric cultures and population movements between the fifth and the third millennia. On the linguistic map, the in-depth study of the diachronic evolution of certain terms has allowed their original meaning to be definitively established. Finally, the rise and development of comparative mythology has allowed the correlation between social structure and the internal hierarchy of the principal pantheons to be illuminated. The names of Marija Gimbutas, Émile Benveniste, and Georges Dumézil — to mention but a few — symbolise these new approaches.

Proto-Indo-European: A Linguistic Fact

The fact of IE is universally recognised today. 'The Indo-European hypothesis has been proven beyond all possible doubt', remarks Paul Thieme.[20] 'If details are still a matter of controversy, the Indo-European hypothesis is most certainly not', adds James P Mallory.[21] It can never be underscored

---

cur over time, this change simultaneously affects all words in the linguistic environment. It was very influential in its time. — Ed.

18   *Elements of the Comparative Grammar of the Indo-Germanic Languages,* 5 vols. (New York: Westermann & Co., 1888–1895. — Ed.

19   Cf. James P Mallory, 'A Short History of the Indo-European Problem', in *JIES,* 1973, pp. 21–65; Calvert Watkins, 'New Directions in Indo-European: Historical Linguistics and its Contribution to Typological Studies', in *Proceeding of the XIIIth International Congress of Linguists,* August 29–September 4, 1982 (Tokyo: The Committee, 1983), pp. 270–277.

20   'The Indo-European Language', in *Scientific American,* October 1958, p. 67.

21   *In Search of the Indo-Europeans: Language, Archaeology and Myth* (London: Thames & Hudson, 1989), p. 22.

enough that the fact of IE is first and foremost a linguistic reality. As Benveniste puts it, 'The Indo-European concept pertains principally as a linguistic concept, and if we can reach to the other parts of culture, it will still be via language'.[22] IE languages, therefore, are those languages presenting common structural traits in phonology, grammar (morphology and syntax), and vocabulary (lexicon). The existence of these languages extends from prehistory to history, traversing all proto-history (which Dumézil[23] qualified as 'ante-history'). All have evolved down to the present day, and continue to evolve. And of course, all bear cultural innovations in the domain of vocabulary and grammar; innovations, however, which obey mechanical constraints orienting them in foreseeable directions. Generally, the IE languages tend to lose their synthetic character over the course of history (complex conjugations, absence or weak use of the article, extremely rich declensions) in order to become more and more analytic (simplification of conjugations, more frequent use of the article and prepositions, impoverishment or disappearance of declensions).

The innumerable homologies and systematic resemblances, as well as lexical, syntactical, or grammatical similitudes that one finds among the IE languages cannot be explained by mere chance or exclusively by loans or sustained contacts. They unite strongly in favour of a common origin. Indeed, the hypothesis of the community of origin is what makes the best sense of the concordances that we find among the linguistic realties characterising languages spoken over an immense territory, ranging from Ireland to Chinese Turkestan.[24] In this hypothesis, the common characteristics of the IE languages are explained by derivation from a unique

---

22   *Le vocabulaire des institutions indo-européennes*, vol. 1 (Paris: Minuit, 1969), pp. 7–8.
     (English edition: *Indo-European Language and Society* [Coral Gables, FL: University
     of Miami Press, 1971]. — Ed.).

23   Georges Dumézil (1898–1986) was a French philologist best known as a pioneer in
     mythography. He also studied the nature of sovereignty in ancient Indo-European
     civilisations, which led him to postulate the Trifunctional Hypothesis: namely,
     that Indo-European culture had developed along a tripartite structure of warriors,
     priests and farmers. He believed that this was the origin of both the Hindu caste
     system and the feudal system in Medieval Europe. — Ed.

24   Cf. NE Collinge, *The Laws of Indo-European* (Amsterdam: John Benjamins, 1985).

language, and their divergences by a separate evolution which has led to differentiation. 'Indo-European', writes Émile Benveniste, 'is defined as a family of languages, issuing from a common language, which have become differentiated by gradual separation'.[25] To say that there is a kinship among IE languages therefore means that if we go back far enough in time, we will find a single primary language from which they all originate, directly or indirectly. This language is called common or Proto-Indo-European (PIE). In a certain sense, Greek, Latin, Germanic, and so on, are simply PIE transformed.

In the strict sense, the term PIE applies only to phonetic, morphological, or lexical protoforms, or even to syntagms, that linguistic palaeontology has been able to reconstruct. By extension, the word designates the language as a whole spoken by the common IE at this stage. The work of linguists has shown that PIE possesses a grammar and a syntax at once complex and relatively homogenous, which prevents it being considered as a mixed language of the creole or pidgin variety. Like the Hamito-Semitic languages, it is a consonantal and inflectional language, in which the lexical sense is expressed by the consonants, whereas the vowels characterise the formation of the inflection: the words generally include an ending indicating their function in the phrase, the nouns and pronouns decline, the verbs conjugate, and so forth. At the last common stage, the verbal system comprised three voices (active, mediopassive, passive), five moods (indicative, subjunctive, imperative, optative, injunctive), and six tenses (present, imperfect, perfect, pluperfect, future, aorist). The inflection includes three numbers (singular, dual, plural), three genders (masculine, feminine, neuter), and eight cases in the inflection of animate gender. Around 4,000 words have been reconstructed to this day.

To explain the formation of the different IE languages, the German philologist August Schleicher (1821–1868), in his 1861 *Compendium der vergleichenden Grammatik der indogermanischern Sprachen*,[26] proposed a

---

25 Op. cit., p. 9.

26 *A Compendium of the Comparative Grammar of the Indo-European, Sanskrit, Greek, and Latin Languages*, 2 vols. (London: Trübner & Co., 1874–1877). — Ed.

model called the 'genealogical tree theory' (*Stammbaumtheorie*), which is still commonly used today. In this model, the essential process is one of divergence: the isolation of a language gradually increases its distinctive characteristics in comparison to other dialects, which differentiate themselves little by little, until they become distinct languages. Schleicher, who was inspired by the theories of Darwin, thought that each language was formed by the separation of an earlier language into two branches. This precludes the possibility that the languages can have contact after diverging from each other. This model was too schematic, which explains why it was criticised in the last century, notably by Max Müller and Hugo Schuchardt.

Another model was proposed in 1872 in a work entitled *Die Verwandtschaftverhältnisse der indogermanischen Sprachen*[27] by the German linguist Johannes Schmidt (1843–1901). This was the 'undulatory' model or wave theory (*Wellentheorie*), and it was based on the idea that at this stage of PIE, there already existed as many dialects as would later become distinct IE languages. All the dialectical differences were therefore already present in the proto-language. For Schmidt, therefore, the IE languages are not differentiated by the migrations of their speakers, but by virtue of the continual growth of the original dialects, without which they would cease to be in reciprocal relation. Whereas in Schleicher's model, the languages detach themselves from each other by successive consequences, in Schmidt's model, they result from an interweaving of isoglosses so complex that it appears futile to trace their genealogy. From this perspective, the well-defined linguistic boundaries implied by the theory of the genealogical tree only result from the disappearance of transitional dialects. With regards to linguistic change, it is propagated like 'waves', provoking convergences which render any recourse to Schleicher's genealogical model unnecessary.

The authors who rally to the model of Schmidt are in general those who hold to an Indo-Europeanisation by progressive contact and ex-

---

27 *Kinship Relations among the Indo-Germanic Languages.* — Tr.

change through a process comparable to that which leads to creole or pidgin speakers. The wave theory was notably used by the Russian linguist NS Trubetzkoy,[28] who in 1936 maintained that all the concordances among IE languages could be explained without making any appeal to the hypothesis of a mother language. This extreme point of view, in which unity realised by a single convergence (*Sprachbünde*), is not supported today by anyone. This also goes for the thesis advanced by Sigmund Feist in 1928, according to which the Germanic languages would represent a sort of 'creolised' IE. The argument that languages have never developed in complete isolation since the Neolithic, and that only 'mixed' languages exist, of which the genealogical tree only gives an inadequate representation, has been retained above all by the Italian 'neolinguistists' from the school of Vittore Pisani and Giacomo Devoto.[29]

28   Nikolai Sergeyevich Trubetzkoy (1890–1938) was a Russian linguist and historian who was instrumental in the development of structural linguistics, and he was also the founder of morphophonology. He was also one of the founding members of the Eurasianist movement among the Russian emigres of the 1920s, and his ideas concerning Eurasia continue to exert influence on Alexander Dugin and his Eurasian Movement in Russia today. — Ed.

29   Cf. Augusto Ancillotti, 'Deep Connections between Indo-European Languages', in *JIES*, Spring–Summer 1995, pp. 113–145, which bases itself on the method of 'selected isoglosses'. Cf. also A Luigi Prosdocimi, 'Diachrony and Reconstruction: *genera proxima* and *differentia specifica*', in *Proceedings of the Twelfth International Congress of Linguists, Vienna 1977* (Innsbruck: Institut für Sprachwissenschaft der Universität, 1978), pp. 84–98; Giuliano Bonfante, 'The Relative Position of the Indo-European Languages', in *JIES*, Spring–Summer 1987, pp. 77–80; Andrew Sherratt & Susan Sherratt, 'The Archaeology of Indo-European: An Alternative View', in *Antiquity*, 1988, pp. 584–595; Stefan Zimmer, *Ursprache, Urvolk und Indogermanisierung: Zur Methode der indogermanischen Altertumskunde* (Innsbruck: Institut für Sprachwissenschaft der Universität, 1990); Stefan Zimmer, 'On Indo-Europeanization', in *JIES*, Spring–Summer 1990, pp. 141–155; and Jean-Paul Demoule, 'Réalité des Indo-Européens: les diverses apories du modèle arborescent', in *Revue de l'histoire des religions*, October 1992, pp. 44–48. The thesis of Troubetzkoy, from a conference announced on 14 December 1936 before the Linguistic Circle of Prague, has been published for the first time in German: 'Gedanken über das Indogermanenproblem', in *Acta linguistica*, 1939, pp. 81–89. The Russian appeared twenty years later: 'Mysli ob indoevropejskoj probleme', in *Voprosy jazykoznanija*, 1959, 1, pp. 65–77 (reprinted in NS Troubetzkoy, *Izbrannye trudy po filologii* [Moscow: Progress Publishers, 1987], pp. 44–59). There is now a French version: 'Réflexions sur le problème indo-européen', in NS Troubetzkoy, *L'Europe et l'humanité: Ecrits linguistiques et paralinguistiques* (Sprimont: Mardaga, 1996),

In the introduction to his book, *Les dialectes indo-européens* (1908),[30] which he wrote in 1903, and which he would revise no less than seven times following this, Antoine Meillet also clearly adopted an anti-Schleicherian position. Following this, however, he supported arguments put forward from 1876 by August Leskien (*Die Declination im Slavisch-Litauischen und Germanischen*),[31] in which the theses of Schleicher and Schmidt were not mutually exclusive. An identical position was adopted by Walter Porzig. As to the problem of the IE dialects, which had been somewhat neglected by the Neogrammarians, it was taken up again in 1925 by Holger Pedersen (*Le groupement des dialectes indo-européens*),[32] followed in 1931 by Giuliano Bonfante, who, in a work consecrated above all to the correspondences between Indo-Iranian and Balto-Slavic (*I dialetti indoeuropei*),[33] went on to become one of the principal opponents of the theory of laryngeals. In the years that followed, the neolinguist Vittore Pisani would present, for his part, a completely revised picture of the distribution of the IE dialects (*Studi sulla preistoria delle lingue indoeuropee*, 1933; *Geolinguistica e indoeuropeo*, 1940).[34]

Strongly criticised by August Fick, who, with essentially phonological arguments, reverted to the 1873 Schleicherian thesis of a derivation by aboresence from a unitary proto-language, the theory of Johannes Schmidt seemed even less convincing after the publication, in the same period, of a study by Heinrich Hübschmann on the place of Armenian among the IE languages. This study demonstrates that the Armenian language is not connected to the Iranian family, contrary to what had

---

pp. 211–230. (There is also an English version: 'Thoughts on the Indo-European Problem', in *N. S. Trubetzkoy: Studies in General Linguistics and Language Structure* [Durham, North Carolina: Duke University Press, 2001] — Ed.)

30   *The Indo-European Dialects* (Tuscaloosa: University of Alabama Press, 1967). — Ed.

31   *Declination in Slavic-Lithuanian and Germanic.* — Tr.

32   *The Family of Indo-European Dialects.* — Tr.

33   *The Indo-European Dialects.* — Tr.

34   *Studies on the Prehistory of Indo-European Languages*, 1933; *Geolinguistics and Indo-European*, 1940. — Tr.

previously been seen in the undulatory theory.[35] The fact that Armenian did not practically exist in a convenient, intermediary state between two families, and that the geographic proximity did not necessarily result in a linguistic proximity, also seems to demonstrate the limits of Schmidt's theory. It is also incapable of explaining peripheral archaisms in a satisfying manner. But properly understood, this does not mean that there were no interactions among the derived languages (areal phenomena). The dominant opinion today is that the undulatory theory retains all its value for the study of IE dialects, but the formation of the IE languages themselves are better explained by the method of the genealogical tree. All the models proposed since the nineteenth century have only served either to weaken or combine those proposed by Schleicher and Schmidt.

Another very important step in the history of IE linguistics has been represented by the theory of laryngeals. The origin of this theory lies in an intuition of the linguist Ferdinand de Saussure[36] about the phonetic state of PIE. In his *Mémoire sur le système primitif des voyelles dans les langues indo-européennes* (1878),[37] Saussure formed the hypothesis that in their origin, all the IE roots began with a vowel possessing a 'quasi-sonant' before this vowel. This initial phoneme would then disappear in the historical IE languages. The hypothesis of Saussure, taken up by the Dane, Hermann Møller, would be confirmed by the inscriptions in Hittite discovered by Hugo Winckler at Boghaz-Köy (ancient Hattusa), which were deciphered in 1914 by Bedrich Hrozny. Jerzy Kurylowicz, a Polish student of Meillet, successfully recognised that some phonetic phenomena from Hittite prove the existence of the 'sonant-vowel' — the ancient common IE phoneme that had disappeared in the other languages, and which has been

---

35   Heinrich Hübschmann, 'Über die Stellung des Armenischen im Kreise der indogermanischen Sprachen', in *Zeitschrift für vergleichende Sprachwissenschaft*, 1875, pp. 5–49.

36   Ferdinand de Saussure (1857–1913) was a crucial figure in the development of linguistics and semiotics, particularly in his identification of what he termed the 'sign', which consists of the signifier (the word used to designate something) and the signified (the image that is produced in the mind upon encountering the word). His work was crucial in the rise of Structuralism. — Ed.

37   *Report on the Primitive Vowel System in Indo-European Languages.* — Tr.

given the name 'laryngeal' since 1911. The 'laryngeal' theories have since continued to multiply.[38] Despite being the object of critiques by those who think their importance is overestimated,[39] they have played a central role in explaining the morphology of PIE, not only in regards to the verbal system,[40] but also in many other domains, such as the reconstruction of the pronominal inflection.[41]

More recently, Thomas V Gamkrelidze and Vjaceslav V Ivanov have also articulated a 'glottalic theory', presenting it as a 'new paradigm' for comparative linguistics.[42] This theory, which rests on a drastic revision and a typological reinterpretation of the entire consonantal system of PIE, allows 'glottalisations' to be reconstructed instead of simple sounds. Since 1973, they have been independently supported by the American linguist, Paul Hopper.[43]

---

38   Cf. Frederik Otto Lindeman, *Einführung in die Laryngaltheorie* (Berlin: Walter de Gruyter, 1970; 2nd rev. ed.: *Introduction to the Laryngeal Theory* [Oslo: Norwegian Univeristy Press, 1987); Edgar C Polomé, 'Recent Developments in the Laryngal Theory', in *JIES*, Spring–Summer 1987, pp. 159–167; Alfred Bammesberger (ed.), *Die Laryngaltheorie und die Rekonstruktion des indogermanischen Laut- und Formensystems* (Heidelberg: Carl Winter, 1988).

39   The neolinguist Giuliano Bonfante went so far as to qualify laryngeals as 'mythic sounds'. Other authors have maintained that the laryngeals were not originally IE, but reflect more a pre-IE substrate. They thus correspond to a mode of adaptation of IE phonetics to the specific pronunciation of pre-IE languages. Discussion otherwise remains open on the exact mumber of laryngeals characteristic of PIE. The most common theory distinguishes three on the basis of internal reconstruction. Other correspondences seem to establish the existence of a labio-velar laryngeal *Aw* and of a palatal laryngeal *Ey* (cf. Jean Haudry, *The Indo-Europeans* [Lyon: Institut d'études indo-européennes, 1994], pp. 13–14).

40   Cf. Calvert Watkins, *Geschichte der indogermanischen Verbalflexion* (Heidelberg: Carl Winter, 1969).

41   Cf. Gernot Schmidt, *Stammbildung und Flexion der indogermanischen Personalpronomina* (Wiesbaden: Otto Harrassowitz, 1978).

42   Cf. Thomas V Gamkrelidze, 'The Indo-European Glottalic Theory: A New Paradigm in IE Comparative Linguistics', in *JIES*, Spring–Summer 1987, pp. 47–59. For a critical point of view, cf. Oswald Szemerényi, 'Recent Developments in Indo-European Linguistics', in *Transactions of the Philological Society*, 1985, pp. 1–71.

43   Cf. Paul Hopper, 'Areal Typology and the Early Indo-European Consonant System', in Edgar C Polomé (ed.), *The Indo-Europeans in the Fourth and Third Millennia* (Ann Arbor, Michigan: Karoma Publishers, 1982), pp. 121–139.

The Debate on the Place of Origin

All language obviously presupposes speakers and bearers: languages do not emigrate, those who speak them do. It is therefore a natural implication that the linguistic notion of IE has also been swiftly employed to designate the speakers of the common proto-language. And just as PIE is a relatively homogenous and unitary language, so too is it concluded, quite logically, that an IE people also existed, also relatively homogenous and unitary, from which the bearers of the historical IE languages derive. This unity is not to be envisioned as a political unity, or even necessarily as an ethnic one, but above all as a cultural unity in the widest sense of the term. 'The unity of language does not assume a political unity any more strongly than an ethnic unity', underscores Georges Dumézil in 1949; 'it attests at the very least to a minimum of common civilisation, of intellectual and moral civilisation, as well as material civilisation'.[44] 'The dominant fact', he would add twenty years later, 'is the community of language, the linguistic unity. Following from this, the elementary understanding that we are willing to make, yet which some still reject, is that such a complete unity cannot go without a minimum of civilisation and of generally mutual conceptions'.[45] Jean Haudry,[46] for his part, specifies that 'the Indo-European linguistic community cannot be that of an empire or confederation; it is necessarily that of a *migrating people*'.[47] Wolfgang Meid summarises the situation in the following terms: 'Every language by definition has speakers, and these

---

44 *L'héritage indo-européen à Rome: Introduction aux séries 'Jupiter, Mars, Quirinus' et 'Les mythes romains'* (Paris: Gallimard, 1949), p. 16. Some years earlier, Dumézil had already emphasised that 'myths are not separable from the whole of the social life' ('L'étude comparée des religions indo-européennes', in *La Nouvelle Revue française*, 1 October 1941, pp. 389–390).

45 Interview with Georges Dumézil, in *Nouvelle Ecole*, September–October 1969, p. 44.

46 Jean Haudry (b. 1934) is a linguist and was a professor of Sanskrit, and was also the founder of the Institute for Indo-European Studies at Jean Moulin University Lyon 3. He was a prominent member of Alain de Benoist's GRECE organisation during the 1970s and was on the Front National's Scientific Council. He has also worked with Terre et Peuple, the group founded by Pierre Vial which also includes the French New Right thinker Guillaume Faye. — Ed.

47 *The Indo-Europeans*, p. 4.

Love, Anika, Dave and Pranidhi

Wishing you the Happiest of Holidays and a wonderful new year!

PEACE

JOY

speakers form a community which, in the case of prehistoric languages, must have lived somewhere, perhaps in different places. And this community must have possessed an identifiable culture that would distinguish it from other communities, language constituting an important aspect of this culture, of which only the surviving materials can be discovered'.[48]

As soon as we admit the existence of an IE people, the question naturally arises: in what manner and on what territory were these people constituted, and where was their previous common habitat located? To these questions, linguistics is not required to respond: it reconstructs PIE, but does not necessarily pretend to retrace the history of its speakers. But this limitation obviously fails to satisfy the spirit. This is because, as soon as the kinship of the IE languages has been recognised, a debate is immediately opened about the geographic location that has been constituted as the original homeland (French *foyer original*, German *Urheimat*) of the IE people. This debate is never closed. It is still open today, even though considerable advances have been made towards a solution. The problem of the origin of the IE languages and of the ethnogenesis of the IE people has been continually agitated by linguists, ethnologists, archaeologists, and cultural historians.

It is primarily in Asia that we have tended to localise this homeland, notably in the Valley of Pamir, the Hindu Kush, or in Turkestan, conforming to the principle *Ex oriente lux*[49] (which Salomon Reinach, in 1893, called 'the oriental mirage') and with an obvious concern to place the discovery of IE in harmony with Biblical scripture. The PIE were thus presented as the descendants of 'Japhet', which would place the root in Asia: in 1767 Parsons published a book entitled *The Remains of Japhet, being Historical Enquiries into the Affinity and Origins of the European*

---

48 'The Indo-Europeanization of Old European Concepts', in *JIES*, Autumn–Winter 1989, p. 298.

49 'Light comes from the east', which has been used to refer to the Orientalists' believe that the most profound human wisdom flows from the Eastern civilisations. — Ed.

Languages. Equally for Herder,[50] the origin of humanity is to be sought in Asia, which Leibniz had already described as '*vagina populorum*'. This thesis has long been reinforced by the erroneous conviction that Sanskrit was the oldest IE language that we could know. In 1808, Friedrich von Schlegel thus described the Indo-Europeans as a 'people of Sanskrit root' [*Völker sanskritischen Stammes*] because he considered Sanskrit as the 'mother-language' of all the others. This opinion, shared by Jacob Grimm, was still alive when Vans Kennedy would publish his *Researches into the Origins and Affinity of the Principal Languages of Europe and Asia* in 1928. The thesis of the Asiatic origin of the IE languages was also adopted by numerous authors of the nineteenth century: Franz Bopp, August Friedrich Pott, Rasmus Rask, Max Müller, August Schleicher, Adalbert Kuhn, Karl Wilhelm Ludwig Heyse, Adolphe Pictet, August Fick, Graziado Ascoli, Henri d'Arbois de Jubainville, William Ripley, Charles Francis Keary, and so on.[51]

Dissenting voices soon made themselves heard. The first to pronounce himself in favour of a European origin of the IE was the German historian, Heinrich Schulz (*Zur Urgeschichte des deutschen Volksstammes*, 1826),[52] followed by the Belgian historian and naturalist, Omalius d'Halloy (1783–1875) who, in 1848, began to refute the thesis of Asiatic origin in a communication presented before the Belgian Academy.[53] In the 1860s, Omalius d'Halloy also became the organiser of a debate on the subject at the Anthropological Society of Paris. In the meantime, the English philologist Robert Gordon Latham (1812–1888) had opined to the same effect, first in an edition of the *Germania* of Tacitus[54] that he published

---

50 Johann Gottfried Herder (1744–1803) was a German philosopher who emphasised the importance of linguistic and geographical differences giving rise to unique identities among nations, thus stressing subjectivity over universality in history. — Ed.

51 This is also, we recall, the opinion of Gobineau.

52 *The Prehistory of the Roots of the German People.* — Tr.

53 Earlier, however, the thesis of the Asiatic origin of humanity had been rejected (in favour of a Nordic origin) by Olof Rudbeck, from Uppsala, in a book entitled *Altland eller Mannheim*, which was published between 1679 and 1698.

54 Publius Cornelius Tacitus (c. 56–c. 117) was a Roman Senator and historian who wrote a number of works, including the *Germania*, which was one of the earliest

in 1851, and then in many of his own works (*The Native Races of the Russian Empire*, 1854; *Elements of Comparative Philology*, 1862). Among his arguments is that it is in Europe, not Asia, where one finds the greatest number of IE languages, suggesting that Europe clearly constitutes the 'centre of gravity'. Like Omalius d'Halloy, Latham supported an original homeland situated in southern Russia, a point of view that would also be adopted by Otto Schrader. This opinion caused him to be mocked in 1874 by Victor Hehn, for whom the Indo-Europeanisation of Europe was the result of nomadic people from Asia (*Kulturpflanzen und Hausthiere in ihrem Übergang aus Asien nach Griechenland und Italien sowie in das übrige Europa*, 1870).[55] 'It is only in England, land of eccentricities', wrote Hehn, 'that someone would think to place the primitive habitat of the Indo-Europeans in Europe'. However, from 1860, the thesis of an Asiatic origin began to encounter massive scepticism.

The 'Germanic' thesis, which situated the homeland in central Germany or in southern Scandinavia, had its first appearance with Lazarus Geiger in 1871. We rediscover it, with various nuances, in Theodor Poesche in 1878, Karl Penka in 1886, and Isaac Taylor in 1888. In 1892, it is taken up with force by Herman Hirt, advocate of an *Urheimat* situated between the Oder and the Vistula, on the shores of the North Sea and the Baltic.[56] Until his death in 1936, Hirt polemicised against Otto Schrader for decades upon this topic.

Unfortunately, considerations foreign to scientific research frequently interfere in this debate. As William Ripley has already said, 'With the possible exception of the theory of evolution, no other subject has been debated with such bitterness, nor has it been obscured in such a diabolical fashion by chauvinist authors full of prejudice'. In Germany in

---

accounts of the Germanic tribes. — Ed.

55 *Cultivated Plants and Domesticated Animals in Their Migration from Asia to Europe* (Amsterdam: John Benjamins, 1976). — Ed.

56 Cf. Herman Hirt, *Die Urheimat der Indogermanen*, 1892; 'Die Urheimat der Indogermanen', in *Indogermanische Forschungen*, 1892, pp. 464–485; 'Die Heimat der indogermanischen Völker', speech delivered 13 July 1891 at the University of Halle/Saale.

particular, the discussion surrounding the homeland would give rise to numerous ideological distortions from the milieu of the Pan-Germanists, who hoped to 'annex' the IE in order to justify their nationalistic pretentions or their desire for conquest using archaeology and linguistics. Such distortions would find their counterparts, also completely utopian, in considerations on the 'linguistic unity' of the human race, or in the works of a V Gordon Childe, who in 1939 presupposed a vast movement of diffusion from East to West described as 'the irradiation of European barbary by Oriental civilisation'. These nationalist preoccupations, rarely presented before the second half of the nineteenth century, are particularly marked among researchers such as Karl Penka[57] (Origines ariacae, 1883; Die Herkunft der Arier, 1886),[58] Ludwig Wilser (Herkunft und Urgeschichte der Arier, 1899),[59] or Gustaf Kossinna[60] (Die deutsche Vorgeschichte, eine hervorragend nationale Wissenschaft, 1911; Die Indogermanen, 1921),[61] founder in 1909 of the review, Mannus, and of the Deutsche Gesellschaft für Vorgeschichte.[62] The 'Germanic' thesis, however, is not always supported by nationalist authors. Hans (Paul) von Wolzogen (1848–1938), for example, who from 1878 became the director of the Bayreuther Blätter,[63] always remained faithful to the thesis of an Asiatic origin. The same was true of Fritz Kern (1927), while Fritz Paudler held to a homeland in the Caucasus. Also, under the Third Reich, a certain number of authors supported perspectives in plain opposition to the official thesis of a purely

---

57 Karl Penka (1847–1912) was an Austrian anthropologist and philologist who first claimed that the Aryan race had emerged in Scandinavia, and that the original Aryans had Nordic features. — Ed.

58 Origins of the Aryans; The Future of the Aryans. — Tr.

59 The Future and Prehistory of the Aryans. — Tr.

60 Gustaf Kossinna (1858–1931) was a German linguist who was the first to identify the Aryan race with the Germans, and his ideas also helped to lay the foundations for a German empire in Europe, as he claimed that the Germans had a right to reclaim all the territories that they had once inhabited. — Ed.

61 German Prehistory, A Preeminent National Science; The Indogermans. — Tr.

62 German Society for Prehistory. — Tr.

63 The Bayreuth Gazette was a newsletter devoted to the ideas and music of Richard Wagner that was published from 1878 until von Wolzogen's death in 1938. — Ed.

Germanic origin.[64] After 1945, we find distortions in the opposite direction
from authors wanting to minimise the fact of IE, which was considered
at the time to be troublesome, embarrassing, or 'politically undesirable'.[65]

64 Hermann Güntert, who was close to the Nazi regime, had always maintained the thesis
of an Asiatic origin of the IE, which was also that of Sigmund Feist (*Kultur, Herkunft
und Ausbreitung der Indogermanen*, [Berlin: Weidmann, 1913]; *Der Ursprung der
Germanen* [Heidelberg: Carl Winter, 1934). The same goes for Victor Hehn. During
the same period, the thesis of a homeland situated in the Pontic steppes, maintained by Otto Schrader contra Herman Hirt and Gustaf Kossinna, was publically
taken up again by Gustav Neckel (*Vom Germanentum* [Leipzig: Otto Harrassowitz,
1944], p. 422). In the meantime, the anthropologist Egon Eickstedt (*Rassenkunde
und Rassengeschichte der Menschheit*, [Stuttgart: Ferdinand Ecke, 1934]) placed the
cradle of the 'Nordids' in Western Siberia during the period of the Würm glaciation. As to Herman Hirt, considerations of a racial nature were always foreign to
him. Conversely, Julius Pokorny, who would emigrate after 1933 after having been
deprived of his chair by the Nazis, never hesitated to call into question the 'racial'
origin of the IE in the 1950s (cf. Ruth Römer, *Sprachwissenschaft und Rassenideologie
in Deutschland* [Munich: Wilhelm Fink, 1985], p. 67). This was equally the case with
Hans Krahe, who also never ceased, under the Third Reich, to criticise the official positions in his reviews for *Indogermanische Forschungen*. We also note that,
in the *Festschrift* published for Herman Hirt in Germany in 1936 (Helmut Arntz,
ed., *Germanen und Indogermanen: Volkstum, Sprache, Heimat, Kultur: Festschrift
für Herman Hirt*, 2 vols. [Heidelberg: Carl Winter, 1936), we find a text by Émile
Benveniste alongside contributions by Otto Reche and Hans FK Günther. On the
connections between archaeology and nationalism, cf. also Margarita Díaz-Andreu
& Timothy C Champion (eds.), *Nationalism and Archaeology in Europe* (Boulder:
Westview Press, 1997).

65 Cf. especially Jean-Paul Demoule, 'Mythes et réalité des Indo-Européens', in *Sciences
humaines*, August–September 1991, p. 53; 'Du mauvais usage des Indo-Européens',
in *L'Histoire*, October 1992, pp. 44–48. Recall also the grotesque *ad hominem* at-
tacks launched against Georges Dumézil by Carlo Ginzburg, Arnaldo Momigliano,
Bruce Lincoln, and so on, to which Didier Eribon has thankfully done justice. 'Like
the accusations of sorcery studied by Mary Douglas', writes Eribon, 'there exists in
the intellectual world the phenomenon of rumour which (...) can cause a scholar
and his work to be burnt at the stake' (*Faut-il brûler Dumézil?* [Paris: Flammarion,
1992], p. 23). On the equally grotesque accusations of 'seizure' [*capitation*] of which
the work of Dumézil was made the object (Maurice Olender, Jean-Paul Demoule,
Alain Schnapp & Jesper Svenbro, etc.), cf. Alain de Benoist, 'Dumézil est-il une sor-
cière?', in *Le Choc du mois*, November 1992, pp. 34–36. Christopher Prescott & Eva
Walderhaug ('The Last Frontier? Processes of Indo-Europeanization in Northern
Europe: The Norwegian Case', in *JIES*, Autumn–Winter 1995, pp. 257–278) recall for their part that, since the 1960s, to evoke the Indo-Europeanisation of the
Scandinavian countries is regarded in Norway as 'politically incorrect', and that the
Swedish edition of the book by Randi and Gunnar Håland on the cultures of prehistory (*Fra Böckers Världshistoria*, vol. 1 [Höganäs: Bra böcker, 1982) could only, for
this reason, be published after having been expunged of its chapters on the Corded

In addition to the authors already mentioned, the 'Germanic' or Nordic thesis has also been upheld by Ludwig Geiger, Matthäus Much, Ludwig Lindenschmidt, Joseph van den Fheyn, Karl Felix Wolff, N Aberg, Franz Specht, Walter Schulz, Hans Seger, Julius Pokorny, Paul Kretschmer, Streitberg, and others. Since 1945 it has been taken up by Nicolas Lahovary, Paul Thieme, Oskar Paret, Hans Krahe, Ram Chandra Jain, Bernfried Schlerath, Lothar Kilian, Alexander Häusler, Carl Heinz Böttcher, and Giuliano Bonfante.

Other authors have placed the original homeland in the current territory of Poland or Lithuania (Harold Bender, Osmund Menghin, Stuart E Mann, Mircea-Mihai Radulescu, János Makkay, Witold Manczak), or even in the Danube region (P Giles, Ernst Meyer, Giacomo Devoto, Milutin and Draga Garasanin, Ronald A Crossland, Igor M Diakonov, Tomaschek).

Since Otto Schrader, Omalius d'Halloy, and Robert Gordon Latham, the 'Pontic' thesis, which situates the IE homeland on the steppes of southern Russia, north of the Black Sea, holds numerous advocates to this day: Salomon Reinach, Sigismond Zaborowski, Albert Carnoy, Harold J Peake, V Gordon Childe, Ernst Wahle, Tadeusz Sulimirski, Georges Poisson, John L Myres, Hans Jensen, Émile Benveniste, Christopher Hawkes, Stuart Piggott, George L Trager, H L Smith, Alexandre Brjusov, Fritz Schachermeyr, Marija Gimbutas, and others.

The Asiatic thesis, by contrast, has remained practically unsupported since the end of the 1930s. Besides Sigmund Feist and his students (Wilhelm Koppers, Alfons Nehring), its principle representatives have been G Sergi, Joseph Widney, Max Müller, Victor Hehn, Jacques de Morgan, Edouard

---

Ware culture. Bernard Sergent, who also denounces the 'calumniators' [*calomniateurs*] of Dumézil, notes for his part that researchers have at all times participated 'in the axiology of their nation or of their epoch' [*de l'axiologie de leur nation ou de leur époque*] (*Les Indo-Européens: Histoire, langue, mythes* [Paris: Payot, 1995], pp. 11 and 37). He does not specify, however, to what 'axiology' he himself adheres. Cf. Dominique Dufresne & Marc Cels, 'Qui a peur des Indo-Européens? Mythologie comparée et probité scientifique', in *Antaios*, June 1996, pp. 174–185.

Meyer, Charles Francis Keary, Henri Hubert, Wilhelm Schmidt, Hermann Güntert, and Wilhelm Brandenstein.

We must finally cite the Near Eastern thesis, which places the original homeland in Asia Minor, or in the territories adjacent to Anatolia and the Aegean. This thesis was notably supported by Benfey, Johannes Schmidt, and Sayce, before being taken up more recently by Gamkrelidze and Ivanov, Aron Dolgopolsky, and Colin Renfrew.[66]

It will be noted that researchers who situate the homeland in the same geographic region have different theses concerning chronology or migration routes. For instance, if we compare the thesis of Renfrew with that of Gamkrelidze and Ivanov, who all situate the homeland in Asia Minor, we see straight away that their views are incompatible, for Renfrew places the dispersion of the IE peoples in the seventh millennium, while Gamkrelidze and Ivanov situate it two millennia later. This difference shows that they are not speaking about the same language or the same people.

Other authors have refrained from participating in this debate altogether. This is notably the case with Georges Dumézil, who, in his first books, only seemed to hold to a northern localisation. In 1924, he described the Celts and the Germans as 'Indo-Eurpoean peoples settled in the North'.[67] Twenty years later, he would evoke a homeland situated somewhere between the Hungarian plain and the Baltic.[68] But generally speaking, the question lies outside his scope: 'On these hotly debated points, the method employed here does not hold, and on the other hand, the solution is of little relevance to the problems posed here. The "Indo-European civilisation" that we envisage is that of the spirit'.[69] At the end of his life, making allusion to the hypothesis of the archaeologist Marija

---

66 We only cite from memory the fantasist locations, such as those that place the origi-
    nal homeland in Africa or further, in an 'Atlantis' identified with the Azores, which
    has also been the Garden of Eden (Karl Georg Zschaetzsch)!

67 *Le festin d'immortalité: Etude de mythologie comparée indo-européenne* (Paris: Paul
    Geuthner, 1924), p. 281.

68 *Jupiter-Mars-Quirinus: Essai sur la conception indo-européenne de la société et sur les
    origines de Rome* (Paris: Gallimard, 1941), pp. 11–12.

69 *L'idéologie tripartie des Indo-Européens* (Brussels: Latomus, 1958), p. 5.

Gimbutas, he contented himself to evoke 'a people more or less unitary, in a domain vast enough for there to have been dialectical differences in a language that they all used. For an unknown reason, thanks to the supremacy of the war horse and the two-wheeled chariot, they expanded in all directions in successive waves, until their reserves were extinguished'.[70]

Archaeology and Linguistcs

Chronology, we come to see, is an essential factor in the debate. As James P Mallory wrote, 'It is completely impossible to test the validity of a theory that seeks to determine *where* the PIE language had been spoken before having determined *when* it had been spoken'.[71] From this point of view, then, linguistics offers little help to researchers. The notion of absolute chronology, familiar to archaeologists, is in effect foreign to them: PIE is a language that is reconstructed solely on the basis of linguistic facts without reference to a given spatio-temporal framework.[72] Because it is unable to take into account the exact chronology of the movements of the located populations and of the resulting cultural contacts, linguistics, despite the valuable indications that it has furnished on the subject, can therefore not clarify the problem of the homeland on its own. Lest it remain purely abstract, the achievements of linguistics must confront those of archaeology.[73]

---

70 *Entretiens avec Didier Eribon* (Paris: Gallimard, 1987), p. 110.

71 'The Indo-European Homeland Problem: A Matter of Time', in Karlene Jones-Bley & Martin E Huld (eds.), *The Indo-Europeanization of Northern Europe* (Washington, DC: Institute for the Study of Man, 1996), p. 1.

72 Cf. the hypercritical remarks of Bernfried Schlerath, 'Ist ein Raum/Zeit Modell für eine rekonstruierte Sprache möglich?', in *Zeitschrift für vergleichende Sprachwissenschaft*, 1981, pp. 175–202.

73 Cf. on this subject Jürgen Untermann, 'Ursprache und historische Realität: Der Beitrag der Indogermanistik zu Fragen der Ethnogenese', in *Studien zur Ethnogenese*, 1985, pp. 133–163; Stefan Zimmer, 'The Investigations of Proto-Indo-European History: Methods, Problems, Limitations', in TL Markey & John AC Greppin, *When Worlds Collide: Indo-Europeans and Pre-Indo-Europeans* (Ann Arbor, Michigan: Karoma Publishers, 1990), pp. 313–344.

Since 1945, the archaeology of Europe has undergone an intense and rapid expansion, furnishing a mass of material data which is sometimes difficult to place in perspective. Above all it has been considerably affected, in the domain of precise chronology, by the radiocarbon revolution (C-14).

From the beginning of the twentieth century, archaeologists were divided between those who adhered to the 'short' or 'traditional' chronology, established in 1905 by Sophus Müller,[74] and those who held to the 'long' chronology proposed the following year, for Scandinavia, by Oscar Montelius.[75] The first was commonly retained in the wake of the First World War, during which it was largely diffused in English-speaking countries under the influence of V Gordon Childe. It proposed a chronology of European protohistory founded upon archaeological relations already acknowledged through the historically datable cultures of ancient Egypt and Mesopotamia. According to the short chronology, the Neolithic cultures associated with IE do not predate the end of the third millennium and the beginning of the second. From this perspective, the European Neolithic commenced late, in the course of the third millennium, and only five centuries separate the first dispersion of IE peoples, around 2500 BCE, and their first historical attestations, around 2000 BCE. In the long chronology, used notably by Richard Pittioni,[76] the European Neolithic dates back, by contrast, to around 5000/4500 BCE, the date of the beginning of the Band Ware culture[77] — the flourishing of the Corded Ware culture[78] being situated in the middle of the third millenium.

---

74 *Urgeschichte Europas: Grundzüge einer prähistorischen Archäologie* (Strasbourg: Karl J Trübner, 1905).

75 *Kulturgeschichte Schwedens* (Leipzig: E A Seemann, 1906).

76 *Die urgeschichtliche Grundlagen der europäischen Kultur* (Vienna: Franz Deuticke, 1949).

77 The Band Ware culture refers to an archaeological period in Europe's prehistory dating to the European Neolithic era which is characterised by its pottery, which lacked handles.

78 The Corded Ware culture is an archaeological period in European prehistory that dates from the late Neolithic through to the early Bronze Age, and traces of it have

Although the first radiocarbon datings began in 1949, the method was only truly established with any strength from the 1960s, when the results obtained from C-14 were able to be 'recalibrated' with data from dendrochronology. The most direct consequence had been to rehabilitate the long chronology, and to turn back the beginning of the Neolithic in Europe to a date much more remote than previously thought. C-14 has allowed us to establish, for example, that the Neolithic began in the British Isles not after 2000 BCE, as Stuart Priggot still believed,[79] but from the beginning of the fourth millennium,[80] and that the complex megaliths of Stonehenge III on Salisbury Plain began to be constructed around 2200 BCE, and not a thousand years later. We also know now that the Kurgan culture[81] may have already formed a distinct entity in the fifth millennium, and that the beginnings of Corded Ware culture date back to the fourth millennium, while those of the Funnel Beaker culture[82] date to the beginning of this same millennium. Simultaneously, numerous cultural phenomena that we had believed possible to attribute to exterior influences reveal themselves much later to be, in reality, autochthonous phenomena.[83] New and

been found all over Northern, Central, and Eastern Europe. It is named after the patterns, resembling cords, which have been found on its pottery. — Ed.

79 *The Neolithic Cultures of the British Isles* (Cambridge: Cambridge University Press, 1954).

80 Cf. Homer L Thomas, 'The Archaeological Chronology of Northern Europe', in Robert W Ehrich (ed.), *Chronologies in Old World Archaeology* (Chicago: University of Chicago Press, 1965), pp. 373–402; *Near Eastern, Mediterranean and European Chronology*, 2 vols. (Lund: Studies in Mediterranean Archaeology, 1967).

81 Kurgan culture designates a number of cultures in Northern and Eastern Europe which existed in the fourth and third millennia BCE. The name comes from the fact that these cultures all left behind kurgans, or mound graves. — Ed.

82 The Funnel Beaker culture designates remnants which have been found in Northern and Central Europe dating to the Copper Age that are characterised by ceramic pieces with funnel-shaped tops. — Ed.

83 Such is the case especially for the great megalithic ensembles of Western Europe, which we once considered as the result of cultural influences coming from the western Mediterranean, and which we today know to antedate the Egyptian pyramids. From 1968, Colin Renfrew, in a sensationalistic article, concluded the chronological impossibility of a Mycenaean influence on the culture or Wessex, whose first tumulus dates from 2100, five centuries before the first tumulus of Mycenaean culture. Cf. 'Wessex without Mycenae', in Colin Renfrew (ed.), *Problems*

refined dating techniques subsequently developed (analysis of pollens,

---

in *European Prehistory* (Edinburgh: Edinburgh University Press, 1979), pp. 281–291. Cf. also Evzen Neustupny, 'Absolute Chronology of the Neolithic and Aeneolithic Periods in Central and South-East Europe, II', in *Archeologické Rozhledy*, 1969, pp. 783–810; Colin Renfrew, *Before Civilization: The Radiocarbon Revolution and Prehistoric Europe* (Cambridge: Cambridge University Press & New York: Alfred A Knopf, 1973); T Watkins, 'Wessex without Cyprus: "Cypriot Daggers" in Europe', in *Festschrift Stuart Piggott*, 1976, p. 136. The previous schematic, which would place the birth of the metallurgy of bronze in Mesopotamia, and which would explain the beginning of the Bronze Age in Central and Southern Europe by influences transmitted from the Near East by Aegean or Anatolian prospectors and traders, has also been abandoned. For continental Europe, carbon-14 dating allows us to situate the first copper foundries in the fifth millennium, in southern Russia, Turkmenistan, and the Transcaucasia, but also in the Carpathian-Balkan sector, and on the territory of the Band Ware culture. These techniques are developed in the fourth and third millennia, especially in Saxony, Thuringia, Schleswig-Holstein (Heligoland), the British Isles, and the Iberian Peninsula, as well as the Unetice culture. The Bell Beaker culture accelerated their diffusion around 2000. We know also that the only objects of true bronze discovered in Asia Minor which are anterior to the Mycenaean epoch come first from the Eastern Mediterranean (Antalya, Soli, Ugarit, Byblos, Troy II), and not from the inside of Anatolia. What is more, while we still believed until recently that bronze metallurgy was not developed in Southeast Asia before the beginning of the first millennium, bronze objects dating from the fourth millennium were found in 1976 in Ban Chiang, in the northwest of Thailand. They would be a thousand years older than the corresponding bronzes of quality discovered as of now in the Near East. The metallurgy of iron is completely different from that of copper and the precious metals by reason of the higher melting point (1535°) which it demands. On the origin of metallurgical techniques, cf. above all the work of Jean R Maréchal, to whom we owe the introduction into France of the spectrographic method: 'Les origines de la métallurgie du cuivre', in *Actes du 81e Congrès national des sociétés savantes*, Rouen-Caen 1956, pp. 119–153; *Zur Frühgeschichte der Metallurgie: Considérations sur la métallurgie préhistorique* (Lammersdorf: Otto Junker, 1962); 'Nouvelles considérations sur l'origine et l'évolution de la métallurgie du bronze', in *Ogam*, July–September 1962, pp. 389–392; 'L'évolution de la métallurgie aux temps préhistoriques', in *Revue de métallurgie*, April 1964, pp. 327–331; 'Nouvelles théories sur l'origine et la propagation du cuivre et de ses alliages en Europe', in *Atti del Congresso internazionale delle scienze preistoriche e protostoriche*, Rome 1965, vol. 2, pp. 370–376; 'Début et évolution de la métallurgie du cuivre et de ses alliages en Europe', in *Janus*, 1970, pp. 1–29; and 'Nouveaux aspects de la métallurgie préhistorique européenne', in *Sibrium*, 1970, pp. 293–303. Cf. also Wilhelm Witter, *Die älteste Erzgewinnung im nordisch-germanischen Lebenskreis* (Leipzig: Curt Kabitzsch, 1938); Wilhelm Witter, *Die Ausbeutung der mitteldeutschen Erzlagerstätten in der frühen Metallzeit* (Leipzig: Curt Kabitzsch, 1938); W Lorenzen, *Helgoland und das früheste Kupfer des Nordens: Ein Beitrag zur Aufhellung der Anfänge der Metallurgie in Europa* (Ottendorf: Niederelbe-H Guster, 1965); and Jacques Briard, 'Les premiers métallurgistes d'Europe', in *La Recherche*, September 1977, pp. 717–725. Colin Renfrew concludes: '[T]he east Mediterranean innovations, which were supposedly carried to Europe by diffusion, are now found earlier in Europe than in the east. The

thermoluminescence, etc.)[84] have confirmed these results.

The obligation to turn back the characteristic sites of European protohistory from 800 years BCE to 2000 BCE has completely transformed our idea of the first waves of IE expansion; at the same time, it constrains us to revise the chronology of the cultures to which these migrations have given birth. After the radiocarbon revolution, it has become impossible to place the dispersion of the original IE community at the end of the third millennium or the beginning of the second (a period recently believed to have coincided with the transition from the Neolithic to the Bronze Age) as we formerly did on the basis of the archaeological dating of the first Anatolian and Hellenistic waves, as well as the study of the Homeric texts and the Vedas.[85] The general conclusion which must be drawn is that the last common habitat of the Indo-Europeans must be sought much earlier in time than we had felt necessary; in other words, at least to the fifth millennium.

A question that remains disputed is the ethnological interpretation of the archaeological material, which has been an object of controversy since the pioneering study of Ernst Wahle.[86] The celebrated 'principle of Kossinna', according to which 'well-delimited archaeological provinces always correspond to the defined people or tribe', is based on the postulate of

---

whole diffusionist framework crashes, and with it the assumptions which sustained prehistoric archaeology for nearly a century' (*Before Civilization*, op. cit., pp. 85).

84 Cf. the results of the Twelfth International Radiocarbon Conference held at Trondheim, Norway, 24–28 June 1985. Cf. also Elizabeth K Ralph & Henry N Michael, 'Twenty-Five Years of Radiocarbon Dating', in *American Scientist*, September–October 1974, pp. 553–560; Robert Hedges, 'New Directions on Carbon-14 Dating', in *New Scientist*, 2 March 1978, pp. 599–601; JR Pilcher & GL Baillie, 'Implications of a European Radiocarbon Calibration', in *Antiquity*, November 1978, pp. 217–221; Paul Aström (ed.), *High, Middle or Low? Acts of an International Colloquium on Absolute Chronology Held at the University Gothenburg 20th-22nd August 1987*, Aström, 1987; and BS Ottaway, 'Radiocarbon: Where We Are and Where We Need to Be', in *Antiquity*, 1987, pp. 135–137.

85 Cf. Homer L Thomas, 'New Evidence for Dating the Indo-European Dispersal en Europe', in George Cardona, Henry M Hoenigswald & Alfred Senn (eds), *Indo-European and Indo-Europeans: Papers Presented at the Third Indo-European Conference at the University of Pennsylvania*, University of Pennsylvania Press, Philadelphia 1970, pp. 199–251.

86 *Zur ethnischen Deutung frühgeschichtlicher Kulturprovinzen* (Heidelberg: Carl Winter, 1941).

an almost mechanical concordance between archaeological remains and linguistic evidence. Not without reason, this principle has been frequently opposed by the possibility of internal evolution or of loans: two peoples speaking the same language can have different material cultures; two peoples sharing the same material culture may not use the same language. A language can also expand by cultural diffusion or by the infiltration of small groups into a new territory, in addition to the migration of the population as a whole. From the archaeological point of view, it follows that we must posit a new culture for a local development if nothing materially attests that it resulted from an invasion. However, if it is imprecise to say that the principle of Kossinna will always be corroborated, it is also completely erroneous to believe that it is always meaningless (no one will contest, for example, that the La Tène culture will be Celtic, or that Jastorf will be Germanic, etc.). Though hostile to Kossinna, Colin Renfrew recognises it himself when he writes that, 'In many cases the archaeological evidence harmonizes well to indicate clear patterns of colonization which satisfactorily account for the linguistic relationships observed.'[87] We generally admit that relative geographic isolation is one of the factors that favour the most linguistic differentiation, above all when it increases by specific features in the domain of material culture. When we find ourselves in the presence of populations where the economy, the funerary rites, the means of construction, pottery, symbols, weaponry, religious beliefs, and so on are mostly different from each other, the likelihood is therefore high that the populations had also spoken different languages.

But one also sees the limitations of archaeology here: it can only provide indications concerning the material culture (economy, technological development, housing, diet, habits of dress, etc.). It certainly contributes to the progress of anthropobiology when it grants the discovery of human remains. It clarifies the social organisation by the study of habitats, graves,

---

87   *Archaeology and Language: The Puzzle of Indo-European Origins* (London: Jonathan Cape, 1987), p. 2.

and funeral rites.[88] It brings to light the locations of cult, thus helping us to better understand the divinities that were honoured. But it can say nothing about the institutions, the intellectual or spiritual life, the language, or the content of beliefs. It occupies itself with tools and dwellings, but remains silent on their deeper meaning. It can, for example, establish a typological link between a pottery style and a class of funerary rite, but it cannot clarify the nature of this link.

Moreover, archaeology is closely dependent on chance findings. A linguistic fact, therefore, cannot always be corroborated by a corresponding archaeological fact. The absence of archaeological data corroborating a conclusion that linguists have arrived at does not mean that the conclusion is meaningless: 'The words inherited from Indo-European are also relics, just as real as archaeological objects, and are sometimes even preserved in a better state'. The presence of IE on the Iranian plateau in the third millennium, for example, is attested by Mesopotamian texts, not by archaeology, and the Creto-Mycenaean civilisation had long been thought to use a non-IE language until the deciphering of Linear-B[89] by Michael Ventris in 1952 demonstrated that the script was written in archaic Greek. Equally, the fact of the reconstructed form *ekwos-, whose single meaning, as attested in seven IE languages, is 'horse', suffices to demonstrate that the IE knew the horse, even if archaeologists have never found any horse skeletons at a European site.

We now understand that linguistics and archaeology have respective strengths and weaknesses. Whereas linguistics studies languages which presuppose speakers, without having the means of dating and precisely situating these languages and speakers, archaeology identifies datable and locatable cultures, without being able to link them to a given language. Archaeology, in the absence of written texts, effectively has no ability to know the language of the humans whose remains they discover. On the

---

88   On the link between social stratification and funerary equipment, cf. C Peebles & S Kus, 'Some Archaeological Correlates of Ranked Societies', in *American Antiquity*, 1977, pp. 421–448.

89   The earliest known form of Greek, dating to the Bronze Age. — Ed.

other hand, if there is no means of linguistically interpreting the results of an archaeological find, it is always possible to search for archaeological traces of an already known linguistic family. As to cultures not directly attested, a necessarily comparative and reconstructive method is followed in order to gain knowledge of them.

The difficulty of matching archaeological data and linguistic data is a traditional obstacle. Each discipline has its methods and its proper rules, and the 'solutions' that they individually advance do not always seem immediately compatible: linguists postulate relations of dialect for which there are no corresponding traces in the movement of peoples, while archaeologists form hypotheses which frequently contradict the linguistic data.[90] Moreover, these disciplines function most often without contact with each other, and the researcher's concern for respectability often causes him to retreat into his speciality when someone asks him what we have every right to expect from him: in this case, of evaluating the degree of probability of the most uncertain or most controversial hypotheses. This explains why the multidisciplinary approach to research is far from dominating the field of IE studies.

'It is completely obvious', said Marija Gimbutas, 'that the solution to the problem of Proto-Indo-European origins, considered on a spatio-temporal basis, finds itself in the hands of archaeologists'.[91] This opinion is highly contestable. To the contrary, despite the complementarity of the two disciplines, priority must indeed be given to linguistics, for the simple reason that it and it alone is necessary to give the very word 'Indo-European' meaning. 'The concept of Indo-Europeans, i.e., of speakers of common IE', writes Vladimir Georgiev, 'is a linguistic one: for this reason the problem of the origin and the original home of the IE languages

---

90   Cicerone Poghirc, 'Pour une concordance fonctionnelle et chronologique entre linguistique, archéologie et anthropologie dans le domaine indo-européen', in Robert Beeks, Alexander Lubotsky & Jos Weitenberg (eds.), *Rekonstruktion und relative Chronologie: Akten der VIII: Fachtagung der Indogermanischen Gesellschaft* (Innsbruck: Institut für Sprachwissenschaft der Universität, 1992), pp. 321–323.

91   'An Archaeologist's View of PIE in 1975', in *JIES*, Autumn 1974, p. 289.

should be examined predominantly through linguistic means and data. However, archaeology, ethnography (ethnology), ancient history, palae-ontology, and anthropology can offer some useful information for finding a solution.'[92] For his part, Aron Dologopolsky remarks, '[I]t is...far from self-evident how archaeologists... can determine *what language* the bear-ers of some Pit Grave culture or Battle Axe culture *spoke*. On the other hand, once the spatial and temporal parameters of the putative homeland have been identified on the basis of *linguistic* evidence, the archaeologists can set about the task of deciding which civilization (archaeologically attested culture or cultures) can be plausibly associated with proto-IE'.[93] János Makkay also affirms that 'in the final analysis, it is obvious that lin-guistics must determine the cultural and geographic parameters of the original Indo-European homeland'.[94] Bernard Sergent underscores that 'the truth of the notion of "Indo-Europeans" is in the language and reli-gion, it is not in the archaeology'.[95]

On the subject that we occupy here, the relation between linguistics and archaeology can therefore be compared to that which exists between an autonomous science and an ancillary science. In regards to the work of linguists, archaeology can and must intervene for the purpose of verifica-tion, when the IE character of a given cultural group has been demon-strated. Its role is to explicate the material data that best corresponds to the findings of linguistics; in other words, to give a palpable reality and an actual chronological dimension to the facts discovered by linguists.

---

92   *Introduction to the History of the Indo-European Languages* (Sofia: House of the Bulgarian Academy of Sciences, 1981), p. 323.

93   'The Indo-European Homeland and Lexical Contacts of Proto-Indo-European with Other Languages', in *Mediterranean Language Review*, 1987, 3, p. 7.

94   'A Neolithic Model of Indo-European Prehistory', in *JIES*, Autumn–Winter 1992, p. 193.

95   Op. cit., p. 394.

Linguistic Palaeontology

The principal method that allows IE to be reconstructed is linguistic palaeontology, also called the 'method of words and things' (*Wörten und Sachen Method*), 'lexico-cultural reconstruction', or 'interpretive etymology'. The expression 'linguistic palaeontology' was created in 1859 by Adolphe Pictet. Based on observations that led to the recognition of the regular nature of phonetic changes, it allows one to restore the elements of the common IE language and, by extension, to conclude from the existence of a word in the vocabulary (*denominans*) the knowledge of the corresponding reality (*denotatum*).

Linguistic palaeontology proceeds either by reconstruction (one compares different elements deriving from several languages in order to reconstruct the term's common origin), or, conversely, it starts from a term common to several languages in order to study the process of diversification that enables new forms to appear. One of the essential principles of this discipline is that all linguistic phenomena common to several IE languages which cannot be identified as loanwords can legitimately be taken as shared IE heritage. This is valid for the isolated sounds (phonemes), the elements involved in the formation of words (morphemes), the isolated words (lexemes), and even the collections of words (phrases), or discursive structures, such as traditional formulas: in general, noun phrases composed from a substantive and an attributive adjective, or from a substantive and a complement in the genitive, of which we know several hundred examples today. Meillet specifies that a word present in at least three IE languages, each of which is separated by other languages, preferably with a distribution from East to West, has the greatest chance of being inherited from IE. These elements must not have been loaned nor translated. (As Paul Kretschmer has indicated, the difference between a loaned term and an inherited term is temporal order: the loaned word reflects a cultural element incorporated at a later date in the common language). Their archaic character must also be demonstrated in order to eliminate the possibility of a spontaneous parallel creation ('elementary parallelism'). Finally, as August Friedrich Pott emphasised at the end of the nineteenth century (and as the Neogrammarians did after him), the form of words counts more than their meaning, for in the process of reconstruction, the laws of phonetics are rigorous, while semantic evolution is unpredictable.

Words attested in at least two languages, in which the phonemes correspond in a regular fashion, and whose senses draw back to the same notion or to the same original situation, are called 'cognates' if their similarity is explained by common inheritance. One of the principal objectives of the comparative method in linguistics is to determine if similar words belonging to different languages are cognates or not. The method employed is based on rules for determining how the phonetic value of a word appearing in the lexicon of one given language is represented in another. Common words like coffee and *café*, for example, are not cognates — they are loanwords made in tandem from Turkish, for it is impossible to reconstruct from them the phonetic form that would have resulted in these terms. A reconstructed IE word is in some respects the residue of a comparison of cognates, that is to say, of a systematic analysis of the grammatical and lexical correspondences based on laws which govern the regular changes of phonetic forms. This comparison takes the form of a simulation of evolutionary processes that could have resulted in the studied forms. From cognates that have the meaning 'hundred' in different languages (Latin *centum*, Avestan *satem*, etc.), one reconstructs, phoneme by phoneme, a common IE word, *$kmtom$- having the same meaning. The reconstruction of the initial letter *k is made possible because the initial phoneme of each cognate derives from a 'k' according to the rules of phonetic transformation characterising the evolution of each of the languages for which we have a cognate. Each phoneme must therefore be compatible with what is known from all the languages that are being compared. When this comparison fails, reconstruction becomes impossible. When it is successful, it allows us to distinguish a reconstructed term whose phonetics have every chance of corresponding to a word that actually exists in PIE.

'Phonetic history is not made with resemblances, but with systems of correspondences', remarks Antoine Meillet. What this means is that, contrary to the beliefs of linguistic amateurs who draw implausible conclusions from simple onomastic approximations or superficial phonetic resemblances, a correspondence that is both linguistic and formal is always more convincing than a purely formal correspondence between terms having different meanings. One could equally say that an isolated lexical identity has barely any meaning by itself, while systematic similarities rarely occur by chance. Vocabulary was the field of language most easily affected by change, and grammatical resemblances are generally regarded as being more significant than lexical resemblances. In addition, loans more often carry the isolated words rather than the morphological elements, such as pronouns, the style of verb conjugation, and so on.[96] 'Morphology', Meillet further emphasises, 'is the most stable thing in language'.[97]

Linguistic palaeontology, whose progress has followed that of general linguistics, is a very secure method. Properly employed, it allows the data for reconstruction to be influenced by a strong coefficient of probability, and it identifies the phases of development in the establishment of the phonological system, the morphology, the syntax, and the lexicon.[98] 'What reconstruction can attain from a linguistic system that has dis-

---

96   Cf. Einar Haugen, 'The Analysis of Linguistic Borrowing', in Anwar S Dil (ed.), *The Ecology of Language: Essays by Einar Haugen* (Berkeley: University of California Press, 1972), pp. 79–109.

97   *The Comparative Method in Historical Linguistics* (Paris: Librairie Honoré Champion, 1967), p. 36. This rule nevertheless undergoes some exceptions. Polish, for example, is closer to Russian than Lithuanian, since Polish and Russian are both Slavic languages, which is not the case with Lithuanian, but this proximity of Polish and Russian seems clearer in the vocabulary than the morphology. Polish is also closer to Ukrainian than Russian, but there are more phonetic resemblances between Russian and Polish than between Polish and Ukrainian.

98   Cf. Wolfgang Meid, 'The Indo-European Lexicon and its Usage as a Problem in Reconstruction', in *Proceedings of the XIIIth International Congress of Linguists, August 29–September 4, 1982, Tokyo*, op. cit., pp. 710–714; and Oswald Szemerényi, 'Recent Developments in Indo-European Linguistics', in *Transactions of the Philological Society*, 1985, pp. 1–71.

appeared', writes Jean Haudry, 'is just as secure as the description of a living language. But it cannot accomplish everything: in particular, the grammatical signifiers (prepositions, postpositions, conjunctions) have a tendency to renew themselves or even to disappear without leaving traces. Reconstruction, whose method is etymological, comes up against this obstacle [...] This is why reconstruction can never be complete. And finally, reconstruction results in forms and structures of different ages, and it is not always possible to establish the chronology'.[99] It is clear, moreover, that in all likelihood PIE contains elements and forms that have disappeared from all IE languages, and can therefore not be reconstructed.[100]

A certain number of words from IE languages apparently cannot be connected to a PIE root. A number of authorities, above all Italian linguists (Bertoldi, Devoto, Gerola, Pieri, Ribezzo, Trombetti, etc.), have observed traces of a pre-IE linguistic substrate. This is not an absurd hypothesis in and of itself, since most IE languages are born from IE populations settling in territories previously inhabited by non-IE peoples. The merging of the two communities logically leaves traces in language. In certain IE languages from the northwest, a greater number of terms and linguistic structures exist which are seemingly underived from PIE, and have therefore been interpreted in terms of a substrate. According to Thomas L Markey,[101] around 28 per cent of the basic Germanic vocabulary is not IE in origin. Enrico Campanile[102] also comes to the conclusion that 28 per cent of the vocabulary of Old Cornish cannot be derived from PIE. Among the phonological traits that could be of non-IE origin in the IE languages of the northwest, Joe Salmons[103] cites the absence of distinc-

---

99   *The Indo-Europeans*, op. cit. (I am unable to find this passage in the English version, Benoist cites p. 6 from the French version. — Ed.)

100 Cf. G Dunkel, 'Typology versus Reconstruction', in *Bono homini donum: Essays in Historical Linguistics in Memory of J. Alexander Kerns*, Amsterdam 1981, vol. 2, p. 563.

101 'The Celto-Germanic "Dog/Wolf"-Champion and the Integration of Pre/Non-IE Ideals', in *NOWELE*, 1988, pp. 3–30.

102 'Indo-European and Non-Indo-European Elements in the Celtic Dialects', in *JIES*, 1976, pp. 131–138.

103 'Northwest Indo-European Vocabulary and Substrate Phonology', in Mohammad Ali Jazayery (ed.), *Perspectives on Indo-European Language, Culture, and Religion:*

tion between the 'a' and the 'o' and the frequent presence of a 'b' at the beginning of words. As the elements are more numerous in Swedish than in Dutch, and in Dutch than in German, one can conclude that north-western Europe had been more superficially Indo-Europeanised than the other regions of Europe which are occupied today by people speaking IE languages, and that it is therefore futile to seek the homeland in this direction. Diverse 'substratic' theories have therefore been proposed, notably concerning the Celtic and Germanic languages.[104] Parallel to this, certain researchers have attempted to reconstruct the pre-IE linguistic elements based on a systematic comparison of all the terms from IE languages that seem impossible to derive from PIE. Such an approach remains largely speculative to the extent that we know nothing of the languages spoken in Europe before the Indo-Europeans. The hypothesis according to which pre-IE Europe had spoken a unitary language, notably supported by Sorin Palinga,[105] who placed the homeland in the Danubian culture of Lepenski-Vir, is both unmanageable and highly improbable. It is more reasonable to think that the Indo-Europeans, in the course of their expansion, met populations speaking very different languages, which were formed and developed over the course of the preceding millennia.

On the other hand, we can ask if the presence of words in IE languages seemingly underived from PIE really carries the influence of a previous substrate, or if this does not simply reflect, at least in a certain number of cases, the present state and current limitations of research. For a long time it was thought that the Greek suffix '-nth-' could be explained by a 'pre-Hellenic' substrate, while today this viewpoint is increasingly under

---

Studies in Honor of Edgar C. Polomé, vol. 2 (Washington, DC: Institute for the Study of Man, 1992), p. 266.

104 Cf. especially Rolf Hachmann, George Kossack & Hans Kuhn, *Völker zwischen Germanen und Kelten* (Neumünster: Karl Wachholtz, 1962); and Wolfgang Meid, 'Hans Kuhns "Nordwestblock" Hypothese: Zur Problematik der Völker zwischen Germanen und Kelten', in Heinrich Beck (ed.), *Germanenprobleme in heutiger Sicht* (Berlin: Walter de Gruyter, 1986, pp. 183–212).

105 'Proto-Indo-European, Pre-Indo-European, Old European: Archaeological Evidence and Linguistic Investigation', in *JIES*, Autumn–Winter 1989, p. 321.

attack. Vladimir Georgiev has even gone so far as to deny the existence of a 'Mediterranean' substrate in the Balkans. A devastating critique of all the substrate theories in Germanic has also been published by Günther Neumann.[106] In the work that he devoted to the IE roots, Norman Bird[107] estimates that most of the terms today presumed to be non-IE or pre-IE have a good chance of being recognised as IE in years to come. Strictly speaking, then, a word that has not yet been successfully connected to PIE cannot be definitively considered as non-IE.

These uncertainties explain why the theories that appeal to a substrate have a bad reputation among linguists.[108] '[S]ubstrate explanations', writes Joe Salmons, 'to the extent that they represent explanations in any strict sense of the word — do remain the vaguest and least supportable arguments in a case where the substrate language is essentially not (directly) attested. For this reason, all other avenues must be exhausted before we reach for a substrate explanation. Substrate explanation for structural features is probable only to the extent that other explanations do not work.'[109] Edgar C Polomé, for his part, has proposed to re-examine the question on the basis of more rigorous criteria.[110] The notion of a 'pre-IE substrate' thus remains fraught with difficulties for now. 'One should not deal with the "substratic" argument', write Christian J Guyonvarc'h and Françoise Le Roux, 'if one does not even know whether the substrate is ethnic or linguistic.'[111]

While the presence in an IE language of terms apparently underived from PIE does not provide a basis for sound conclusions, the absence of any term of this kind from a given section of the lexicon is significant by contrast. This observation forms the basis of theses developed, from the

---

106 *Substrate im Germanischen?*, Wiesbaden 1982.

107 *The Distribution of Indo-European Root Morphemes: A Checklist for Philologists* (Wiesbaden: Otto Harrassowitz, 1982).

108 Cf. Sarah Grey Thomason & Terrence Kaufman, *Language Contact, Creolization, and Genetic Linguistics* (Berkeley: University of California Press, 1988), pp. 111–112.

109 Art. cit., p. 266.

110 'Substrate Lexicon in Germanic', in *NOWELE*, 1989, pp. 53–73.

111 *La civilisation celtique* (Paris: Payot, 1995), pp. 17–18.

1930s and '40s, by Hans Krahe regarding North European hydronymy.[112] We know that hydronyms count among the best-preserved names over the course of millennia. Krahe, after Jan Rozwadowski (1913), found that the part of Europe comprising the region between southern Scandinavia and the northern border of the Alps on one hand, and between Ukraine and the Netherlands on the other, was the only place on the entire continent where the hydronyms were always without exception IE in origin. He concluded that this region is where PIE had been formed, or at least that it had been occupied by the IE speakers from very ancient times. From the correspondences between the names of rivers in Baltic, Germanic, Celtic, Italic, and so on, he was also able to assert that the languages must have formed a linguistic unity north of the Alps. Krahe would initially interpret the linguistic unity for which the hydronyms provided testimony in light of the 'Illyrian'[113] hypothesis, since he gave it the name 'Old European' (vieil-européen, alteuropäisch). Although it has been criticised, notably by Hans Kuhn in 1967, this point of view retains its full value to this day. Reformulated by Krahe in the 1950s after abandoning the 'Illyrian' hypothesis,[114] it was taken up in more recent times by Wolfgang P

---

112 Hydronymy is the study of river names, or hydronyms. — Tr.

113 The hypothesis from the late 1930s that made 'Illyrian' a major component of the Indo-Europeanisation of Europe has been abandoned today. From this perspective, Indo-Europeanisation is largely identical to the diffusion of the Lusatian and Urnfield cultures. Hans Krahe further assimilates the Proto-Illyrians to the 'People of the Sea and the North' (including the Philistines) mentioned in Egyptian documents. Cf. Hans Krahe, 'Der Anteil der Illyrier an der Indogermanisierung Europas', in Die Welt als Geschichte, 1940, pp. 54–73; and Die Indogermanisierung Griechenlands und Italien, (Heidelberg: Carl Winter, 1949). Today the term 'Illyrians' only applies to the populations that established themselves in the southeast part of Dalmatia.

114 Cf. Hans Krahe, Sprachverwandtschaft im alten Europa (Heidelberg: Carl Winter, 1951); Sprache und Vorzeit: Europäische Vorgeschichte nach dem Zeugniss der Sprache (Heidelberg: Quelle & Meyer, 1954); Vorgeschichtliche Sprachbeziehungen von den baltischen Ostseeländern bis zu den Gebieten um den Nordteil der Adria (Wiesbaden: Franz Steiner, 1957); 'Indogermanisch und Alteuropäisch', in Saeculum, 1957, 1; and 'Vom Illyrischen zum Alteuropäischen: Methodologische Betrachtungen zur Wandlung des Begriffes "Illyrisch"', in Indogermanischen Forschungen, 1964, pp. 201–213.

Schmid,[115] who extended the region studied by Krahe to Western Russia. Vladimir Georgiev, for his part, had extended it to the Balkan Peninsula. According to Schmid, there is no doubt that the hydronyms of this region are directly connected to PIE, and he adds that it is in the Baltic region that one can best identify them. It is, in effect, only in the territories where the Baltic languages are spoken that one notes a perfect continuity between the 'old-European' background and the historically attested languages. This observation argues for a very ancient settlement of the Balts in their historical territory, and leads one to believe that the Baltic lands could have been the centre of diffusion of the hydronyms in question.[116] The 'old-European' hydronymy attests in every case to a definite linguistic continuity in this region. The question remains open as to whether 'old-European' merges itself with PIE (which appears most probable), whether it should be seen as a secondary linguistic group, or even an IE language that is extinct today. The existence of an IE hydronymy (and also of an IE toponymy) between the North Sea and the Vistula, in the Alps, the Balkans, and Ukraine, is also one of the arguments upon which Lothar Kilian bases himself in order to situate the last common IE habitat on this territory.

Words and Things

As has been said above, linguistic paleontology allows us to deduce from the existence of a common IE word the knowledge of its corresponding reality. However, this conclusion only has an indicative value, and the passage from one to the other no longer appears as obvious today as it did a century earlier. In effect, the lexical method has some limitations: in the strict sense, a lexeme gives nothing but a lexeme. In this domain too, the gains of linguistics must also be corroborated, whether with the cultural

---

115 *Alteuropäisch und Indogermanisch* (Mainz: Akademie der Wissenschaften und der Literatur & Wiesbaden: Franz Steiner, 1968); and 'Baltische Gewässernamen und das vorgeschichtliche Europa', in *Indogermanische Forschungen*, 1972, pp. 1–18.

116 Cf. on this subject Heinz-Dieter Pohl, 'Le balte et le slave', in Françoise Bader (ed.), *Langues indo-européennes* (Paris: CNRS Editions, 1994), pp. 233–250.

context, or the data of archaeology.[117] The Dumézilian method, from this point of view, is already a textual reconstruction, in other words a comparison of contents. The recourse to etymology is also enlightening. It can indicate what appears to be the major characteristic or quality of the thing designated by the term. For example, there are two names designating the noble metals in IE languages: one is related to the IE root *arg- and means 'brilliant white', and the other to the IE root *ghel-, 'yellow', and, assuming we did not know already, this immediately tells us which name corresponds to silver and which to gold. This approach also has its limits, however. One cannot always deduce the functional concordance from the lexical concordance: that the common IE name for the king, *re:g- finds itself in Sanskrit (ra:j-), Latin (rex), Gallic (rix), and Irish (ri), does not mean that the Latin king had the same rights and obligations as the Celtic king.[118] Conversely, we know that gods carrying completely differ-

---

117 Cf. Enrico Campanile, 'Reconstruction culturelle et reconstruction linguistique', in Françoise Bader (ed.), Langues indo-européennes, op. cit., pp. 25–41.

118 We know that the information on royalty among the IE is particularly complex. The common IE name for king, *re:g-, seems to have first designated 'he who draws the (straight) line', who embodies that which is 'right' or 'straight', who indicates the direction to follow. Jan Gonda gives the root from which this word derives the primary meaning of 'extend' [étendre], in the sense of 'to protect or guard' [protéger], then 'to direct' [diriger]. Other interpretations have been advanced, notably by A Shiler ('The Etymology of PIE *reg-, "King" etc.', in JIES, 1977, pp. 221–246), which suggests the meaning of 'effective (religious) power'. The fact that many words of the same origin belong to the religious domain has also lead Vendryès and Benveniste to conclude that the IE king originally had an essentially religious function. The exclusively religious role of rex in the Roman Republic could therefore be an archaism. In any case, the IE conception of royalty evolved very early (cf. Georges Dumézil, L'idéologie tripartie des Indo-Européens, op. cit., pp. 32–33). Royalty in the martial sense appears to be a recent phenomenon. The use of the word 'king' even seems somewhat anachronistic for the common IE period, where society was essentially organised in chiefdoms, that is, in autonomous groupings of a certain number of families and clans (cf. Ralph M Rowlett, 'Archaeological Evidence for Early Indo-European Chieftains', in JIES, Autumn–Winter 1984, pp. 193–233; and S O'Brien, 'Social Organization in Western Indo-European', in JIES, 1980, pp. 123–163). We can only speak of 'royalty' in the ordinary sense of the word when authority ceases to be exercised on the basis of kinship bonds alone, becoming more properly 'political' (proto-feudal) than tribal. Furthermore, the birth of this political royalty has sometimes led to the appearance of a new term (in Ireland, for example, where brenin is substituted for ri).

ent names (Aphrodite and Venus, Hera and Juno, etc.) can be functional counterparts, and also that IE divinities could bear non-IE names (which was frequently the case in Greece). Due to the constant renewal of vocabulary in this domain (and also, sometimes, of the 'secrecy' surrounding the names of the gods), not a single name of a PIE divinity has been able to be reconstructed in a satisfying manner — with the exception of the name of the diurnal Sky, his sons the divine twins, and some celestial bodies or divinised natural phenomena. Finally, apart from the danger that the presence of a word, seen from a grammatical model, can result from a diffusion or a loan, as is often the case in regions that practice bilingualism, we must still account for the fact that an inherited word could have received different meanings in different languages. The difficulty is then to determine what the original meaning is. Not all linguists follow Émile Benveniste, for instance, when he postulates that the primary meaning of the PIE term *peku-, 'livestock', was 'moveable goods, transportable property'.

In spite of excessive critiques more suited to paralysing research than stimulating it, which we can address,[119] the method of 'words and things' nevertheless reveals an incontestable fecundity. In furnishing information both about things and the way in which these things have been interpreted or viewed, it is particularly significant when they are applied to groups of terms, or even to entire fields. Far from being reduced to a simple language game, reconstruction allows us to gain information concerning the IE that archaeology is incapable of providing.

For reasons which have already been made clear (the possibility that a common term in the derived languages has been lost), the fact that we have not been able to reconstruct a PIE word for a thing does not necessarily mean that the Indo-Europeans did not know this thing;

---

119 Cf. for example Bernfried Schlerath, 'Können wir die indogermanische Sozialstruktur rekonstruieren? Methodologische Erwägungen', in Wolfgang Meid (ed.), *Studien zum indogermanischen Wortschatz* (Innsbruck: Institut für Sprachwissenschaft der Universität, 1987), pp. 249 ff.; and Stefan Zimmer, 'Indogermanische Sozialstruktur? Zu zwei Thesen Émile Benvenistes', ibid., pp. 315 ff.

rather, it only shows the limitations of the research. Although we have not reconstructed a common word for 'hand', for instance, we can assume that the Indo-Europeans already had hands! We have also struggled to reconstruct a word for 'fur' or 'hair'. We have common names for 'eye' and for 'eyebrow', but not for 'eyelid'. That we have not been able to reconstruct a common word for 'husband' or 'wife' doesn't mean that the Indo-Europeans did not know marriage. The common IE name for 'man' (Latin *homo*) is no longer found in Russian. We also know that certain terms have been made the object of taboos. This is notably the case with the she-bear, which is most often designated by paraphrases ('the destroyer', 'the brown one', 'eater of honey', etc.), and also for the liver (due to its use in certain divination techniques). The negative argument, *ex silentio*,[120] therefore has demonstrative value for some isolated words. Nonetheless, it is perfectly convincing when it applies itself to a series of related words or to words connected to a whole field. The absence of common IE terms for Mediterranean flora and fauna, for example, show that it is highly unlikely that the homeland was situated in Southern Europe: that there is no common IE word for grapevine, palm, laurel, cypress, olive, and so on shows that the IE were not originally from a Mediterranean region.[121] IE also does not have a common word for donkey; and yet the donkey was known very early in Mesopotamia.

Jürgen Untermann[122] has shown that the common IE vocabulary completely refutes the idea that the PIE were a nomadic people. We also know that there were no nomadic peoples between the Dnieper and the Ural between the fifth and third millennia, only pastoral populations. The mode of life of the IE most likely combined a pastoral lifestyle with sedentary, agrarian work, along with a practice of transhumance within

---

120 Latin: 'argument from silence'. — Ed.

121 The efforts deployed by Vladimir Georgiev to demonstrate that the IE knew the vine, the cypress, and olive oil from the etymology of the corresponding Greek words is not convincing.

122 'Ursprache und historische Realität: Der Beitrag der Indogermanistik zu Fragen der Ethnogenese', in *Studien zur Ethnogenese*, 1985, p. 161.

a small radius. Study of the lexicon shows that the principal occupation involved raising livestock, possession of which was a symbol of wealth, as testified by the relationship of terms designating livestock (IE *peku-) with silver (pecuniary), and numerous mythic accounts dealing with cattle raiding.[123] We also find common names for 'mutton', 'goat', 'pig', and 'dog', which demonstrate that the final habitat did not exist prior to 5000 BCE, the date at which the first economies of the Neolithic type appeared in the temperate zone. On the agricultural plane, the IE notably cultivated grains, including barley and wheat. As Johannes Hoops and Herman Hirt have shown, despite arguments which oppose Victor Hehn and Otto Schrader, they knew the plough, whose name (Vedic si:ra, Tocharian are, Armenian arwar, Greek arotron, Latin aratrum, Old Icelandic ardhr, Common Slavic *ordlo, Lithuanian árklas, Middle Irish arathar, etc.) derives from a root *arH3-, meaning 'to plough, work the earth' (Greek aroô, Latin aro, arare, Middle Irish airim, Gothic arjan, Lithuanian ariù, and without doubt also Hittite harsh-).[124] One also finds the common IE words for 'mill' and 'grindstone', but not for 'bread'. The IE used the chariot; they practiced spinning and weaving, as well as beekeeping. There is no common word for 'bee', but there is one (*melit-) for 'honey' (Tocharian B mit, Lithuanian medús, Latvian medus, Old Prussian meddo, Old Irish ái, etc.), whence Balto-Slavic *medhu-, an intoxicating brew made from honey (cf. English mead). The term designating metal, *áyes-, derived from *-e/os-, from the root *ay-, 'to heat, set on fire', with the original sense of 'heating' (cf. Sanskrit ayas, Avestan ayo, Latin aes, Gothic aiz, etc.), refers to copper and bronze (a copper reinforced by arsenic or tin). We can infer that the final period of the IE community was situated after the invention of the copper of metallurgy, but before that of iron.

---

123 Cf. Bruce Lincoln, 'The Indo-European Cattle-Raiding Myth', in History of Religions, 1976, pp. 42–65; and Boris Oguibenine, 'Le symbolisme de la razzia d'après les hymnes védiques', in Etudes indo-européennes, April 1983, pp. 1–17. Without a doubt, the word *péku- first designated woolly livestock, from which we get fleece (*pék-e/os-), before it applies to other classes of domestic animals.

124 Cf. Gy Wojtilla, 'Notes on Indo-Aryan Terms for "Ploughing" and the "Plough"', in JIES, Spring–Summer 1986, pp. 27–37.

Herman Hirt, Sigmund Feist, Otto Schrader, Giacomo Devoto, and Émile Benveniste have applied themselves to the task of reconstructing the IE system of kinship. Modern authors who have weighed in on the problem[125] generally estimate that the system was of the Omaha III type, that is to say, it was a patriarchal, patrilineal, and patrilocal system, functioning on the basis of marriages between cross cousins. Study of the possessive pronoun in PIE also shows that property was not individual, but belonged to the extended or joint family, of which the *zadruga* of the southern Slavic populations is perhaps a survival.[126] One of the characteristic traits of the Omaha system is avuncularism. The grandfather and the mother's brother, in other words the maternal uncle, are assimilated to the extent that we use the same word to designate them (cf. Latin *avunculus*, literally 'little grandfather'); the same goes for the grandson and nephew (IE *nepot-, 'nephew', the basis of Latin *nepos-* and Old High German *nefo*, 'grandson').[127] The custom of marriages between cross cousins, resulting in the fact that the brother of the mother of the mother is the same person as the father of the father, explains the privileged position

---

125 Cf. Floyd G Lounsbury, 'A Formal Account of Crow—and Omaha—Type Kinship Terminologies', in Ward H Goodenough (ed.), *Explorations in Cultural Anthropology: Essays in Honour of George Peter Murdock* (New York: McGraw-Hill, 1964); Paul Friedrich, 'Proto-Indo-European Kinship', in *Ethnology*, 1966, pp. 1–36; Franck Joseph Florian Wordick, *A Generative-Extensionist Analysis of the Proto-Indo-European Kinship System, with Phonological and Semantic Reconstruction of the Terms* Dissertation, University of Michigan at Ann Arbor 1970; H Gates, 'The Kinship Terminology of Homeric Greek', in *International Journal of American Linguistics*, 1971; and R Keesing, *Kin Groups and Social Structure* (New York: Holt Rinehart & Winston, 1975), pp. 112–120. Martin E Huld ('CuChulainn and his IE Kin', in *Zeitschrift für Celtische Philologie*, 1981, pp. 238–241) thinks that the IE kinship system was in fact of the Omaha II or IV type. R Beekes ('Uncle and Nephew', in *JIES*, 1976, pp. 43–63) and Oswald Szemerényi ('Studies in the Kinship Terminology of the Indo-European Languages, with Special References to Indian, Iranian, Greek and Latin', in *Acta Iranica*, 1977, pp. 1–240) are almost the only ones to reject any assimilation to Omaha type systems.

126 Cf. John W Richards, 'The Slavic "Zadruga" and Other Archaic Indo-European Elements in Traditional Slavic Society', in *The Mankind Quarterly*, Spring–Summer 1986, pp. 321–337.

127 Cf. also Archie C Bush, '"Nepos" Again', in *JIES*, Autumn–Winter 1987, pp. 285–296, who maintains a different point of view.

accorded to the maternal uncle, which Tacitus has described among the Germanic peoples,[128] and of which one still finds traces today.[129] It is difficult to know whether this IE kinship system is entirely original or if, as Benveniste thinks, it preserves the trace of a previous system practicing matrilineal descent, which it might have concealed.

The IE root *do:- means 'to give', but in Hittite da- means 'to take, receive'. We can also compare German nehmen, 'take' and Greek nemo, 'to give, provide', or English 'give' and Irish gaibid, 'take'. This double meaning shows that the IE practiced the gift and counter-gift as described by Marcel Mauss. The ambivalent character of relations with the stranger is similarly attested by the common word *(g)hosti-, which forms the basis of both 'host' (French hôte) and 'hostile' (Latin *hostis, 'enemy'). Bernard Sergent, for his part, emphasises that 'in all the ancient IE societies, war is the principal activity'.[130]

The works of Georges Dumézil on functional tripartition are sufficiently known as to not require review here. After having believed that the tripartite system, which was recognised in 1938, 'after fifteen years of painstaking trial and error',[131] represented the projection of a genuine ancient division of society into three classes, Dumézil ceased, in around 1950, to believe that this trifunctionality had always been a social and political reality, and instead began to recognise it as a system of thought, a scale of values.[132] Sergent defined this system as an 'exhaustive provisional

---

128   De Germania, 20: 'The sons of sisters receive from their uncle the same respect as their father' [sororum filiis idem apud avunculum qui apud patrem honor].

129   Cf. German Oheim, 'oncle', a word which Rudolf Much derived from common Germanic *auhaim- and, beyond this, from IE *awos koimos, 'kind grandfather'.

130   Op. cit., p. 282.

131   Georges Dumézil, Gods of the Ancient Northmen (Berkeley: University of California Press, 1973).

132   Cf. Georges Dumézil, Mythe et épopée I: L'idéologie des trois fonctions dans les épopées des peuples indo-européens (Paris: Gallimard, 1968), p. 15. We note that some of the disciples or admirers of Dumézil, in particular some historians of Roman law, have not followed him in his evolution. Cf. Jacques Ellul, 'Recherches sur les conceptions de la souveraineté dans la Rome primitive', in Mélanges offerts à Georges Burdeau, 1977, p. 336.

analysis of the characteristics of the world'. The three functions do not necessarily correspond to three differentiated classes: the tripartite ideology does not automatically result in tripartite institutions. In the historical period, neither Rome nor the Germanic world presented a division into three classes, and nothing authorises us to think that such a division was present in common IE society, especially in its origin. From this point of view, the reoccurrence of the three functions is the High Middle Ages represents an ideological resurgence more than an institutional survival.

The Indo-Europeans honoured the celestial divinities and knew the two meanings of the word 'sacred' ('that which carries a sacred presence' and 'that which is forbidden'), but it is difficult to know whether they possessed a sacerdotal caste. That the existence of such a caste is only attested at the extremes of the IE sphere (Brahmans and Mazdaean clergy in the East, Celtic druids and Roman flamines in the West), and that this is also where the IE name of the king *re:g- had been preserved, whereas it had disappeared in the 'central' zone (among the Germanic, Balto-Slavic, Greek, and Scythian peoples), has occasionally been explained by the conservative and 'archaising' character of the peripheries.[133] Other authors, by contrast, see this as a later stage. Although Caesar affirms that the Germans had no 'druids', Tacitus, in numerous instances, indicates otherwise: that the priests play an important role in Germanic political and religious life. Jan de Vries[134] also believes that equivalents of the Gallic triad of druids, bards, and ovates must have also existed among the Germanic peoples. But actually, the Germans seem to have been specialists of the cult more than a true sacerdotal caste.

The existence of the IE poet is, however, well attested. Here we have a professional whose social role is highly significant: the poet conveys a global ideology in the form of a semiotic system of formulas to be memorised (signs of relations between things, traditional conceptualisations, etc.) The ancient texts compare him to a 'carpenter', because he joins

---

133 Cf. Georges Dumézil, *Apollon sonore et autres essais* (Paris: Gallimard, 1982), p. 226.
134 *Kelten und Germanen* (Bern: Francke, 1960), p. 90.

words together like pieces of roofing, as is attested in the association of the IE substantive *wékwos, 'speech', and the root *teks-, 'to work wood', which forms the basis of the word *text* (French *texte*) (*wékwos teks-*, 'to construct the expression'). The existence of a common IE poetic formula was established during the nineteenth century by Adalbert Kuhn in a celebrated article on 'immortal glory' published in 1853. From the phonological point of view, IE verse includes several phonetic features, such as rhythm and alliteration. It also holds an initiatic aspect, based on a 'secret language' or an enigmatic play of words, of which the Germano-Scandinavian *kenningar* (kennings) are a continuation.[135]

The name of the 'sea' (French *mer*) poses a difficult problem. A common word, *mori*, is attested in several languages, but the debate as to its primary meaning is still open. Some estimate that this word originally meant 'marsh'. We fail to see, however, regardless of what hypothesis might be accepted concerning the location of the homeland, how the IE could not have known either the North Sea or the Baltic Sea, neither the Caspian Sea nor the Black Sea, especially since there are words for 'oar' and 'boat' (*ná:w-*). The Greek word for 'sea', *thalassa*, is apparently not of IE origin, which suggests that the early Greeks came from a continental region. The Germanic vocabulary pertaining to the sea (English *sea*, German *See*) was considered to be non-IE by Sigmund Feist,[136] who also translated *mori* as 'marsh'. Krzysztof Tomacz Witczak[137] deems to the contrary that 84 per cent of the terms from this vocabulary are 'autochthonous', and that 59 per cent of them are from words of IE origin. He concluded that the Germanic peoples had known the sea and seafaring since the remotest of times. Herman Hirt suggested that some IE peoples could have lost the

135 Cf. Rüdiger Schmitt (ed.), *Indogermanische Dichtersprache* (Darmstadt: Wissenschaftliche Buchgesellschaft, 1968); and Calvert Watkins, 'Aspects of Indo-European Poetics', in Edgar C Polomé (ed.), *The Indo-Europeans in the Fourth and Third Millenia*, op. cit., pp. 104–120.

136 *Indogermanen und Germanen* (Halle: Max Niemeyer, 1914).

137 'The Pre-Germanic Substrata and Germanic Maritime Vocabulary', in Karlene Jones-Bley & Martin E Huld (eds.), *The Indo-Europeanization of Northern Europe*, op. cit., pp. 166–180.

word during the course of their movement to the interior of the European continent.

The reconstruction of common IE words for snow, ice, wolf, and bear (*Hrktos*), as well as beaver (Avestan *bawri-*, Latin *fiber*, Cornish *befer*, Old High German *bibar*, etc.) show that the IE people lived in a cold or temperate climate.[138] They knew mountains, plains, rivers, and lakes. We have reconstructed the common words for spring, summer, and winter, but not for autumn. The trees most familiar to them were the beech, ash, oak, birch, aspen, willow, walnut, hazel, and so on.[139] Based on the IE lexicon of the flora and fauna, a longstanding traditional approach has been to compare the results obtained with clues supplied by paleobotany and paleozoology. We believed that we could identify the initial dispersion zone, but this approach reveals itself to be somewhat discouraging, as shown by the discussion that took place regarding the beech and the salmon.

We had first thought that the IE name of the 'salmon' *laksos* (Anglo-Saxon *lax*, German *Lachs*, and Russian *lossos*) designated the Atlantic salmon, which would suggest that this fish was absent from the rivers which flow into the Caspian Sea, the Black Sea, or the Mediterranean, situating the source of the homeland in a region irrigated by the rivers that flow into the North Sea or the Baltic. Paul Thieme puts forth an argument situating the homeland on the plain of north Germany. However, the fact that the word *laks* means 'fish' in Tocharian, and that in Sanskrit *laksa* has taken the sense of '100,000, a very large number' has led us to ask: what is the original meaning of the term? Some authors have asserted that it might have originally related to different kinds of fish, salmonoid or near salmonoid, encountered by the Indo-Europeans in various regions of

---

138 On the non-domestic animals known by the IE, cf. the exhaustive panorama established by James P Mallory, 'Indo-European and Kurgan Fauna I: Wild Mammals', in *JIES*, Autumn–Winter 1982, pp. 193–222.

139 Cf. Paul Friedrich, *Proto-Indo-European Trees: The Arboreal System of a Prehistoric People* (Chicago: University of Chicago Press, 1970).

Europe or Asia. For A Richard Diebold, Jr.,[140] *laksos could have originally designated the salmon trout (*Salmo trutta labrax* or *Salmo trutta capsius*), which we find in abundance in the rivers of regions situated north of the Caspian and Black Sea. Gamkrelidze and Ivanov have identified it as the *Salmo trutta aralensis*, which is found in the Aral Sea. In addition, we cannot find a convincing IE etymology for the name of the 'eel' (common Germanic *e:la-).[141] The same goes for the name of the 'herring' (common Germanic *he:ringaz).

Because the beech (Latin *fāgus*, Germanic *boka*, German *Buche*) only grows in Western Europe from Königsberg to Odessa, Paul Thiery put forth an argument situating the homeland on the plains of north Germany, between the Elbe and the Vistula. The same argument had been used by Lazurus Geiger in 1870, and was taken up again by Karl Penka and Herman Hirt. Identical reasoning has been held regarding the birch (German *Birke* < Old High German *birihha*, 'white tree'). Johannes Hoops[142] also remarked that the names of trees growing in central and northern Europe are rediscovered in most of the IE languages; he drew the conclusion that the original homeland must be sought west of a line linking Prussia to Turkey. A similar hypothesis was held by R Braungart,[143] which asserted the plains of northern Europe as well. However, it should be noticed that in Greek, *phègos* designates not a beech, but a species of oak with edible acorns, and that in Russia, a word of the same origin designates the elder (elderberry). As for the Kurdish word *buz*, believed to designate the beech, it refers in reality to the elm. Finally, in Albanian, a word derived from IE *bhagos* is used to designate the chestnut, whereas the beech is designated by a word (*ah*) derived from the IE name for the ash, *okso-*. Such facts prevent us from knowing with certitude which tree

---

140 *The Evolution of Indo-European Nomenclature for Salmonid Fish: The Case of 'Huchen' (Hucho Spp.)* (Washington, DC: Institute for the Study of Man, 1985).

141 Cf. Jan de Vries, *Nederlands etymologisch woordenboek* (Leiden: EJ Brill, 1977, p. 1.

142 *Waldbäume und die Kulturpflanze im germanischen Altertum*, Strassburg 1905.

143 *Die Urheimat der Landwirtschaft aller indogermanischen Völker und der Geschichte der Kulturplanzen und Ackerbaugeräte in Mittel- und Nordeuropa nachgewiesen* (Heidelberg: Carl Winter, 1912).

was originally designated by *bhagos*. However, the common IE name of the silver birch, *bhergo-*, a tree genuinely characteristic of northern Europe, finds itself in almost all the IE languages. Derived from a verbal root meaning 'to shine, become white' (the bark of the birch is white), it is attested in the Slavic, Baltic, Italic, Germanic, and Indo-Iranian languages, where it regularly means 'birch', except in Latin, where a form derived from it (*fraxinus*) means ash.

All together, these considerations show that it is difficult to identify the original homeland based solely on terms concerning flora and fauna, and that we must also take into account mitigating climactic variations in Europe over the course of the millennia that preceded our era. In the best case, paleaobotany and palaeozoology only allow us to eliminate hypotheses which place the original homeland outside of Europe. These methods are more difficult to use in order to distinguish between authors who place it in different locations within the European continent. They do not offer any indication of chronological order: to know that the IE knew the oak is only currently of interest from a geographical point of view, since this tree has been present in Europe since the Middle Cretaceous. In the in 1950s, Hans Krahe declared that it was better to abandon, at least temporarily, the arguments of the beech, the birch, and the salmon.

If we summarise the data concerning the chronology furnished by linguistic palaeontology, we note that the dispersion of the PIE from their last common habitat could not be earlier than 5500/4500 BCE. The presence of common words for pottery, domestic animals, and certain forms of agriculture effectively prevent us from tracing this dispersion back before the Neolithic (what is not permitted, however, is placing the formation of language later).

As to the lower limit (the *terminus ante quem*),[144] it evidently corresponds to the earliest historical attestations of an IE language. Some Anatolian proper names of IE origin had already been mentioned around 1900 BCE in Akkadian and Hurrian commercial texts. The oldest exist-

---

144 Latin: 'the latest possible date'. — Ed.

ing IE inscription, the text of Anitta, has been preserved on a tablet from the seventeenth century BCE. It includes mention of a god Shius, who is no other than the god of the diurnal sky (IE *dyeus).[145] Hittite is attested by Cuneiform documents from the sixteenth century BCE. The Hittite archives, discovered in 1907 by the archaeologist Hugo Winckler on the site of Boghaz-Köy, deliver the text of a treaty completed around 1380 BCE between the Hittite king, Supiluliuma, and the king of the Mitanni, Matiwaza — which also contains the name of many divinities — as well as numerous technical terms related to horse-breeding appearing in a Hittite treatise composed by an 'Arya' of the Mitanni. What stands out from these diverse indications is that the IE languages from Anatolia were already well established at the beginning of the second millennium. The Indo-Europeans seem to have penetrated into Anatolia later, around 2700/2600 BCE.[146] Taking account of the necessary time for the differentiation of languages, this lets us suppose that the Anatolian languages had detached from the common trunk much earlier. What is more, it is probable that these languages (Hittite, Luwian, Palaic, etc.) had already differentiated themselves before their speakers arrived in Asia Minor. The prevailing opinion today, which is notably based on the archaism of the Anatolian

---

145   Cf. Erich Neu, Der Anitta-Text (Wiesbaden: Otto Harrassowitz, 1974).

146   We unfortunately know nothing of the prehistory of the Hittites. Gerd Steiner ('The Role of the Hittites in Ancient Anatolia', in JIES, Spring–Summer 1981, pp. 150–173) thinks that their entry into Anatolia must go back to the fourth millennium, and that the Luwians had succeeded them in the second half of the third millennium. This entry was effected from the east (Akurgal, Kammenhuber, Otten, Schmökel, von Soden, Sommer), the west (Cavaignac, Cornelius, Gelb, Coetze), the northeast (Bittel), or from the Black Sea (Bin-Nun, Gurney). The most likely hypothesis is that of a penetration from the west, for in the absence of useable archaeological data, it is that which best corresponds to what we know of the direction followed by the IE languages in Asia Minor and of the diffusion in relation to the non-IE languages of the region. Cf. Gerd Steiner, 'The Immigration of the First Indo-Europeans into Anatolia Reconsidered', in JIES, Spring–Summer 1990, pp. 185–214. Cf. also Ferdinand Sommer, Hethiter und Hethitisch (Stuttgart: W Kohlhammer, 1947); Eugène Cavaignac, Les Hittites (Paris: Adrien Maisonneuve, 1950); Annelies Kammenhuber, Die Arier im Vorderen Orient (Heidelberg: Carl Winter, 1968); Friedrich Cornelius, Geschichte der Hethiter (Darmstadt: Wissenschaftliche Buchgesellschaft, 1973); and Kurt Bittel, Die Hethiter (Munich: CH Beck, 1976).

group, is that the process of dialectisation of the proto-language that results in Anatolian emerged as early as the fourth or fifth millennium.

Archaic Structures

Lexicostatistics alone does not obviously suffice to determine the relationships among the IE languages.[147] It is also necessary to compare their
structure and their general morphology. It has been observed, chiefly
since the 1930s, that the most peripheral IE languages are also those that
have preserved the greatest number of archaic linguistic and religious
facts. Some linguists have derived a theory in which archaisms preserve
themselves better at the periphery, whereas innovations are more frequent
in the central area. However, for Antoine Meillet, this phenomenon is explained more simply by the fact that the peripheral languages were the
first to break away from the common trunk. In this view, these languages
therefore represent a more ancient phase of PIE. The discovery of Hittite
and Tokharian, whose archaic characteristics are well established, has led
in every case to lending PIE a new dimension of depth; at the same time,
it constrains the comparativists to situate themselves in more dynamic
perspectives.

While the verbal system of Greek or Sanskrit is extremely rich, since
it contains three voices (active, middle, and passive), four modes (indicative, subjunctive, optative, and imperative), and four tenses (present, aorist, future, and perfect), the verbal system of Hittite only contains two
voices (active and mediopassive), two modes (indicative and imperative),
and two tenses (present and praeterite). It does not distinguish well between the present and the past, and forms its imperative from the present.[148] Hittite knows the distinction between the singular and the plural
forms, but does not know the dual. Its nominal system, which makes no
distinction between masculine and feminine, only contains two genders,

---

147 Cf. Dell Hymes, 'Lexicostatistics so Far', in *Current Anthropology*, 1960, pp. 3–44.
148 Cf. Hisanosuke Izui, 'Indo-European Perfect and Hittite Verbal System', in *JIES*,
      Autumn–Winter 1986, pp. 195–204.

the common gender and the neuter. Other characteristic traits of Hittite are the mediopassive in '-r-' (as in the Baltic languages), the preservation of laryngeals, the inflected type called 'heteroclitic' (of which traces no longer exist in other IE languages), some special pronominal forms, and so on.

These particularities, in connection with the other observations made in the religious and social domains (in addition to the linguistic data, we note the absence in Hittite of the traditional IE formula), have led us to ask whether Hittite preserved an archaic verb and noun system, a system of which Greek and Sanskrit represent the most recent forms, or if, to the contrary, it is plausible that the verb and noun system of PIE could have been partially 'lost' in Hittite, but preserved in Greek and Sanskrit. The fact that Hittite is the most anciently attested IE language already pleads in favour of the first hypothesis, which is ultimately revealed to be correct. In fact we find no traces in Hittite of anything which suggests that it could have possessed other linguistic features at an earlier period, other than those of which we already know. The idea that Hittite is merely a deformed IE, 'Creolised' under the influence of non-IE languages from Asia Minor, has also been abandoned. The Hittite linguistic system does not appear to have been influenced by Semitic languages or by non-IE Anatolian languages.[149] It does not know the dual, for example, which would have logically been preserved if it had undergone the influence of Semitic languages. Finally, Hittite shows affinities with the majority of other IE languages, which allows us to presume that it existed for a long time in the area of the IE protolanguage. The conclusion that the majority of researchers have sustained is that Hittite 'lost' nothing of the IE linguistic system and that it did not result from a simplification of a more complex, ancient system, but rather that if reflects, to the contrary, one of the most ancient forms of PIE, which leads us to believe that it

---

149 Cf. Annalies Kammenhuber, 'Hethitisch, Palaisch, Luwisch und Hieroglyphenluwisch', in *Handbuch der Orientalistik: Altkleinasiatische Sprachen* (Leiden: EJ Brill, 1969), pp. 119–357.

broke away from the common stem at a particularly remote date.[150] Hittite therefore constitutes a particularly valuable testimony concerning the original IE community: it lets us know what the characteristic traits of PIE were in an epoch where, for example, the language only distinguished between the animate gender (which would evolve into the masculine and feminine genders) and the inanimate gender (which would give birth to the neuter). It is even possible that the Anatolian branch was the first to separate from the last common IE habitat, and this might mean that it is necessary to assume a previous original habitat different from that which we have postulated for the other Indo-European peoples. We also recall that it is on the basis of the archaism of Hittite that Edgar H Sturtevant, in the 1930s, was able to advance the hypothesis — still controversial this day — of an 'Indo-Hittite' protolanguage.[151]

Another particularly interesting case is that of Tocharian, an IE language spoken at a very remote time in Chinese Turkestan. We have given the name 'Tocharians' to its speakers in reference to the historical *Tocharoi*, which the Greeks knew to have emigrated from Turkestan into Bactria during the second century of our era. But this denomination is erroneous: the true Tocharians, or (Eteo-Tocharians) are the East Iranians. The

---

150 Cf. Wolfgang Meid, 'Probleme der räumlichen und zeitlichen Gliederung des Indogermanischen', in Helmut Rix (ed.), *Flexion und Wortbildung: Akten der V. Fachtagung der Indogermanischen Gesellschaft* (Wiesbaden: Ludwig Reichert, 1975), pp. 204–219; and 'Der Archaismus des Hethitischen', in Erich Neu & Wolfgang Meid (eds.), *Hethitisch und Indogermanisch: Vergleichende Studien zur historischen Grammatik und zu dialektgeographischen Stellung der indogermanischen Sprachgruppe Altkleinasiens* (Innsbruck: Institut für Sprachwissenschaft der Universität, 1979), pp. 159–176. WP Lehmann, Warren Cowgill, Erich Neu, William R Schmalstieg, Edgar H Sturtevant, Wolfgang P Schmid, B Rosenkranz, etc. significantly come to the same conclusions. An opposing point of view is maintained by Heinz Kronasser, *Vergleichende Laut- und Formenlehre des Hethitischen* (Heidelberg: Carl Winter, 1956), p. 163; and *Etymologie der hethitischen Sprache, I,* (Wiesbaden: Otto Harrassowitz, 1966). On the Hittite language, cf. also Johannes Friedrich, *Hethitisches Wörterbuch* (Heidelberg: Carl Winter, 1952); and Emmanuel Laroche, *Catalogue des textes hittites* (Paris: Klincksieck, 1971).

151 Cf. Edgar C Sturtevant, *A Comparative Grammar of the Hittite Language* (Philadelphia: Linguistic Society of America, 1933; 2nd ed.: New Haven: Yale University Press, 1964); and *The Indo-Hittite Laryngeals* (Baltimore: Linguistic Society of America, 1942).

word *tougrien* was also proposed, but gained little success. The Tocharian language divides itself into two groups: Tocharian A, or East Tocharian, spoken in the region of Agni to the East of current Chinese Turkestan, with Turpan and Karachar as principal centres; and Tocharian B, or West Tocharian, which was more ancient, spoken above all in the Kuchean region, and which eventually supplanted the other. Their speakers designated themselves respectively under the names Arśi and Kuči, whence the name 'Arśi-Kuči group' given to them by Bernard Sergent. The first manuscripts in the Tocharian language that have come down to us date to the sixth to eighth centuries of our era. They were deciphered at the beginning of the twentieth century by Emil Sieg and Wilhelm Siegling, who, in an article regarded as the birth of 'Tocharology',[152] recognised them as an IE language. The Tocharian cultures disappeared after the ninth century with the entry of the Uyghur Turks into China, who brought about the collapse of the local kingdoms.

The deciphering of the Tocharian language has allowed us to confirm an IE presence in this region of the world, however remote it may be from Western Europe. The recent discovery of the 'mummies' of the Tarim Basin[153] shows that this presence dates back to at least the beginning of the second millennium. Some authors have concluded that the Tocharians, or other groups of IE origin established early in the north of China, could have played a role in the birth of Chinese civilisation, a hypothesis already advanced in the nineteenth century by the French Orientalist, Terrien de La Couperie. In 1924, Hubert Schmidt asserted that the most ancient Chinese cultures were of IE origin. In 1926, O Franke identified the Tocharians with the founders of the first Chinese Dynasty,

---

152   'Tocharisch, die Sprache der Indoskythen', in *Sitzungsberichte der Berliner Akademie der Wissenschaften*, 1908, pp. 915–932. The first results of the deciphering of the language were presented the same year before the Berlin Academy. Cf. also Hückel, 'Une nouvelle langue indo-européenne', in *Revue des études anciennes*, July–September 1909.

153   Lop Nur, in the Tarim Basin of northwestern China, is the site of the Xiaohe Tomb complex, which is a Bronze Age burial site that dates to about 4000 BCE. It was first identified by archaeologists in 1934. — Ed.

ARCHAIC STRUCTURES 53

the Xia Dynasty (2200–1750 BCE).[154] But we do not know exactly where the Tocharians came from. If we admit a very early separation of this group, it is possible that the Afanasevo culture,[155] situated near the Altai Mountains, represented a step on its path towards the East. It is also possible that the Tocharians were first guided towards the Balkans, following the Anatolians, before resuming their route towards the East after being in contact with the Proto-Greeks. Some authors have seen the Guti, whose presence is attested in Mesopotamia in the third millennium, as the ancestors of the Kuči. Oswald Menghin thought it possible that the Tocharians had initially inhabited Ukraine, where they developed the last phase of

154 Cf. also Williams, 'The Origin of the Chinese', in *American Journal of Physical Anthropology*, 1918, pp. 183; Richard Wilhelm, *A Short History of Chinese Civilization* (New York: Viking, 1929); O Kümmel, 'Die ältesten Beziehungen zwischen Europa und Ostasien', in *Deutsche Forschung*, 1929, p. 115; JG Andersson, 'Researches into the Prehistory of the Chinese', in *Bulletin of the Museum of Far Eastern Antiquities*, 1943; and EG Pulleyblank, 'Chinese and Indo-Europeans', in *Journal of the Royal Asiatic Society*, April 1966, pp. 9–39. On the first Chinese dynasties, Xia and Shang, cf. Jean-Paul Desroches, 'La naissance de la civilisation chinoise', in *La Recherche*, September 1973, pp. 761–770; Kwang-chih Chang, 'The Origin of the Chinese Civilization: A Review', in *Journal of the Oriental Society*, 1978, pp. 85–91; and Kwang-chih Chang, 'In Search of China's Beginnings: New Light on an Old Civilization', in *American Scientist*, March–April 1981, pp. 148–160. The Chinese word **mjit*, 'honey', has a good chance of being derived from Tocharian B *mit*, which has the same meaning. The very significant similarities that we have been able to detect between the IE religion and the structure of the Japanese Shinto pantheon, established at the beginning of the ninth century in *Kojiki* and *Nihon Shoki*, do not result from a Tocharian influence, but is more likely explained by the Scythian or Sarmatian myths transmitted from the Eurasian continent to the Japanese archipelago through the Altaic pastoral culture and the Korean Peninsula. The excavations undertaken in the royal sepulchres of Korea testify to an undeniable Scythian influence (who were themselves in contact with Hellenistic culture) upon the ancient Korean culture, in particular during the Kofun period, between the end of the third century and the middle of the sixth century CE. Cf. Atsuhiko Yoshida, 'Mythes japonais et idéologie tripartite indo-européenne', in *Diogène*, April–June 1977, pp. 101–124; and Taryo Obayashi, 'La structure du panthéon nippon et le concept de péché dans le Japon ancien', ibid., pp. 125–142. On the possible affinities of the IE languages with Korean, cf. Koppelmann, 'Die Verwandtschaft des Koreanischen und der Ainu-Sprache mit den indogermanischen Sprachen', in *Anthropos*, 1928, p. 199; and *Die eurasische Sprachfamilie: Indogermanisch, Koreanisch und Verwandte* (Berlin: Weidmann, 1934).

155 Afanesevo culture designates remnants that have been identified in southern Siberia, the oldest yet discovered, dating to about 3500–2500 BCE. –Ed.

the Cucuteni-Trypillian culture before penetrating into China, but this hypothesis seems highly unlikely.

It is principally on the linguistic plane, however, that Tocharian has reserved some surprises. While it was expected that this language would be related to the Indo-Iranian dialects, with which it has, on the contrary, only very little in common, we have observed that it bears traits characteristic of the Celtic and Germanic languages, and furthermore, that it presents certain similarities with Hittite. Proto-Tocharian, from which Tocharian A and Tocharian B derive, additionally belongs to the group of languages called *centum*, along with Hittite, Greek, Latin, the Germanic, Italic, and Celtic languages, and not to the *satem* language group, to which it should *logically* belong due to its geographic location.[156] Finally, Tocharian pre-

---

156   *Cent* (hundred) is pronounced as *känt* in Tocharian A and *kante* in Tocharian B. The distinction between the '*centum* languages', which maintain the dorsal occus-live (**k* and **g*), and the '*satem* languages' (like Armenian, Albanian, Indo-Iranian, the Slavic and Baltic languages), which transform them into palato-alveolar frica-tives, sibilant spirants, or affricates, has long been considered to reflect an ancient bifurcation of the IE linguistic community. Franz Bopp, who first made this dis-tinction in 1853, thought that this difference in phonetism reflects the most ancient separation occurring inside PIE, and that the separation of the Balto-Slavs and the Indo-Iranians, realised by the departure of the former, occurred at a period later than the migrations of the IE *centum* group. The distinction was next taken up by Karl Brugmann (*Elements of the Comparative Grammar of the Indo-Germanic Languages*, 1886) and Peter von Bradke (*Beiträge zur Kenntnis der vorhistorischen Entwicklung unseres Sprachstammes*, Gießen 1889), followed by the whole school of 'Neogrammarians'. In 1954, Walter Porzig (*Die Gliederung des indogermanischen Sprachgebiets*, [Heidelberg: Carl Winter, 1954]) further classed the IE languages into a West group and an East group according to these criteria. This classification was called into question when it was realised that we can only group languages accord-ing to their geographic distribution alone, and that if we consider the treatment of the consonantal series, we are led to completely different groupings. Furthermore, the distinction *centum/satem* divides closely related languages in a completely arbi-trary fashion, such as Germanic and Balto-Slavic. We also know that Greek, which is connected to the *centum* group since it preserves the dorsal occlusive, is also related to the *satem* group by the fact that it changes them into sibilants (as in Russian) or into palato-alveolar fricatves (as in Sanskrit). Vladimir I Georgiev is among those who have most aptly revealed the superficial character of this opposition, from which we have today ceased to deduce anything of broad scope. It remains that the *centum* character, due to the fact that the ancient labiovelar occlusives remain distinct whereas the palatals and the pure velars amalgamate, could be linked to an archaic stage of PIE, while the *satem* character would correspond to an innovation.

sents a significant number of archaisms,[157] which leads us to believe that it detached itself from the common trunk, if not during the same epoch as the Anatolian group, then at least shortly thereafter. From here, the most diverse hypotheses have been issued. Meillet feels that the PIE dialect that gave birth to Tocharian is situated between the 'Italo-Celtic' dialect and the Slavic and Armenian dialects. Julius Pokorny has underscored the resemblance of Tocharian to Armenian and Thraco-Phrygian. Holger Pedersen, in 1923, defended its affiliation with the northwest group of IE languages, basing his hypothesis on significant terms, such as the Tocharian name for 'fish', *laks*, and on the existence in Tocharian A of a verb, *sary*, 'to sow'. In 1936, Benveniste declared that 'Tocharian is an old member of a prehistoric group (to which Hittite also perhaps belongs), which borders on Baltic and Slavic on the one hand, and Greek, Armenian, and Thraco-Phrygian on the other'. Other authors have emphasised the common traits existing between Tocharian and Slavic (the fact, for example, that IE *eu* regularly transforms itself into *-yu-*). Bernard Sergent feels that 'the ancestors of the Arśi-Kuči must have dwelt among the ancestors of the Germans and the ancestors of the Balto-Slavs'.[158] The dominant opinion is that Tocharian is a 'northwestern' language proper that separated very early from PIE, and in this regard it deserves to be compared to the Anatolian languages.[159]

Tocharian and Hittite are not the only languages that present an archaic character. The archaism of the Baltic languages, in particular Lithuanian, has been emphasised by Herman Hirt since 1892. It has also

---

157 The archaic character of Tocharian has been established notably by Holger Pedersen, RA Crossland, Francisco Rodriguez Adrados, Gamkrelidze, and Ivanov. Cf. also JHW Penney, 'Preverbs and Postpositions in Tocharian', in *Transactions of the Philological Society*, 1989, pp. 54–74.

158 Op. cit., p. 113.

159 Cf. especially Douglas Q Adams, 'The Position of Tocharian among the Other Indo-European Languages', in *Journal of the American Oriental Society*, 1984, pp. 395–402, which above all reconciles Tocharian with Germanic. Donald R Ridge, 'Evidence for the Position of Tocharian in the Indo-European Family?', in *Die Sprache*, 1990, pp. 59–123, expresses a more doubtful point of view. For an overview of recent findings: Bernfried Schlerath, *Tocharian: Akten der Fachtagung der Indogermanischen Gesellschaft* (Reykjavik: Malvisindastofnum Haskoka Islands, 1994).

been emphasised more recently by Wolfgang P Schmid in the context of his work on hydronyms, which we have already mentioned. In the case of the Baltic languages, one such archaism could plead in favour of a homeland in the region where these languages developed. We can note, furthermore, that Lithuanian possesses a highly developed declension system, which includes no less than eight different cases (nominative, vocative, accusative, genitive, ablative, dative, locative, and instrumental). Some archaisms specific to the Slavic languages have also been listed by Meillet.

Germanic also presents archaic traits, among which we can cite the late preservation of laryngeals, the absence of the durative past (imperfect) and doubtless also the aorist, some traits of nominal and prenominal inflections, and so on. The similarity of the verbal systems in the Germanic and Anatolian languages has been emphasised by Jean Fourquet: the only difference is that Germanic also includes an optative used as a conjunctive. Wolfgang Meid and Erich Neu, to whom we owe the elaboration of the pattern of diachronic development of the IE verbal system,[160] have also noted the kinship on this point of the Germanic and Anatolian languages. However, contrary to that of Hittite, the verbal system of Germanic appears to preserve vestiges of two other tenses, which it subsequently lost. Such facts suggest that the Proto-Germanic peoples separated themselves from the common trunk at an early date, when they already used the optative, but not yet the praeterite, in other words at a time when the complete system of verbal inflection, as we observe it in Greek and Indo-Iranian, has still not appeared.[161] In addition to numerous archaisms of the lexical order, this hypothesis allows us to explain the absence of the aorist and the fact that Germanic does not make the distinction between the

---

160 Cf. Erich Neu, 'Zur Rekonstruktion des indogermanischen Verbalsystems', in Anna Morpurgo Davies & Wolfgang Meid (eds.), *Studies in Greek, Italic and Indo-European Linguistics, Offered to Leonard Palmer on the Occasion of His 70th Birthday* (Innsbruck: Institut für Sprachwissenschaft der Universität, 1976), pp. 239–254.

161 Cf. Edgar C Polomé, 'Isoglosses and the Reconstruction of the IE Dialectal Split', in *JIES*, Autumn–Winter 1994, p. 300.

perfect and the imperfect, the subjunctive and the optative.[162] According to Edgar C Polomé, the Germanic tribes had been among the first to leave the original homeland, which prevented them from knowing subsequent developments in the verbal system. Germanic must therefore be considered as the most ancient western IE language; Greek and Indo-Aryan are by contrast the most recent.[163] This point of view is also confirmed by the 'glottalic theory' of Paul Hopper. It denies the theory that Germanic had ever formed a 'Creolised' language, a *Mischsprache*, as Sigmund Feist had purported,[164] followed more recently by Witold Manczac. However, there exists an incontestable pre-IE substrate in Germanic, which German authors have often falsely denied, but the most recent works show that it has been completely integrated into the language.[165]

Evolution of the Language and Glottochronology

The issue of knowing how and in what order the IE languages have progressively differentiated themselves from each other still remains one of the most controversial questions today. The scope of the evolution of a language depends in part on its extent over time; a specialised discipline, glottochronology, has given itself the task of evaluating the rhythm of the evolution of languages in the hope of being able to date the moment that

---

162 Cf. Edgar C Polomé, 'Prehistoric Linguistic Contacts in Northern Europe and their Reflexes in the Lexicon', in *Lingue e culture in contatto nel mondo antico et altomedievale* (Brescia: Paideia, 1993), p. 47.

163 Cf. Edgar C Polomé, 'The Dialectal Position of Germanic Within the West-Indo-European', in *Proceedings of the XIIIth International Congress of Linguists*, op. cit., p. 741. Cf. also Matteo Bartoli, 'Il carattere arcaico dei linguaggi germanici', in *Archivio glottologico italiano*, 1938, pp. 52–68.

164 'The Origin of the Germanic Languages and the Indo-Europeanization of North Europe', in *Language*, 1932, pp. 245–254.

165 Cf. Wolfgang Meid, 'Bemerkungen zum indogermanischen Wortschatz des Germanischen', in Jürgen Untermann & Bela Brogyanyi (eds.), *Das germanische und die Rekonstruktion der indogermanischen Grundsprache* (Amsterdam: John Benjamins, 1984), pp. 91–112.

they diverged from each other suffiently enough to give birth to distinct languages. Tadeusz Milewski[166] thus affirms that the different IE dialects existing around 1500 BCE must have nurtured connections with PIE analogous to those which the different Romance languages of our day maintained with their Latin ancestor fifteen centuries ago. He deduces that the IE linguistic community began to disaggregate around 3000 BCE. Warren Cowgill[167] adopts the same approach, believing that the differentiation between Greek, Anatolian, and Indo-Iranian could not have taken more than two thousand years, but not less than a thousand, which brings the date of the last stage of common IE back to 3500/2500 BCE. Morris Swadesh[168] proposes to shift this date back to 4500/4000 BCE. All hypotheses nevertheless remain largely speculative, which explains why the claims of glottochronology have been frequently debated.[169] One of its foundational postulates is that languages effectively evolve according to a constant rhythm; the 'linguistic clock' to which glottochronology makes appeal is in this regard comparable enough to the 'molecular clock' used by biologists to evaluate the evolution of genetic frequencies.[170] Linguists, despite their efforts, could never establish strict rules concerning the rhythm and extension of linguistic changes. The rhythm of evolution and

---

166 'Die Differenzierung der indoeuropäischen Sprachen', in *Lingua Posnaniensis*, 1968, 12–13, pp. 37–54.

167 Warren Cowgill & Manfred Mayrhofer, *Indogermanische Grammatik I: Lautlehre* (Heielberg: Carl Winter, 1986), pp. 69–70.

168 'Unas correlaciones de arqueologia y linguistica', in Pedro Bosch-Gimpera (ed.), *El problema indoeuropeo* (Mexico: Universidad autonoma de México, 1960), pp. 343–352.

169 Cf. especially Andrée F Sjoberg & Gideon Sjoberg, 'Problems in Glottochronology', in *American Anthropologist*, 1956, pp. 296–300; Knut Bergland & Hans Vogt, 'On the Validity of Glottochronology', in *Current Anthropology*, 1962, pp. 115–153; A Richard Diebold Jr., 'A Control Case for Glottochronology', in *American Anthropologist*, 1964, pp. 987–1006; and István Fodor, *The Rate of Linguistic Change* (The Hague: Mouton, 1975).

170 Cf. Luca L Cavalli-Sforza, *Genes, Peoples, and Languages* (New York: North Point Press, 2000), pp. 216–220, who extends the analogy by comparing the efforts of linguists reconstructing an IE proto-language to those of biologists comparing DNA sequences of different species when investigating the likelihood of a common ancestral sequence.

of the differentiation of language has varied according to the importance of populations, of their geographic isolation, of contacts which have favoured or impeded lexical innovations, the erosion of meaning, borrowings, and so on. As a result, the data of glottochronology can rarely be used literally, especially since it leads to estimations of such magnitude that one cannot contest them: knowing that the first dispersion was situated between 4500 and 2500 BCE, which almost the entire world admits, does not allow us to narrow down the diversity of existing hypotheses.

Since the nineteenth century, most researchers have admitted that the geographic distribution of the different IE languages essentially reproduces those of the IE dialects that gave birth to them: Indo-Iranian to the east, Celtic to the west, Balto-Slavic to the north, and so forth. In addition, the geographic distribution of languages sometimes accords with the their structural relationship: Portuguese looks more like Spanish than Catalan; Spanish more like Catalan than Provencal; Catalan more like Provencal than French, and so on. However, these rules, which Meillet has already cast doubt upon, carry exceptions: although attested very much to the east of the spectrum of IE expansion, Tocharian is nonetheless a 'western' IE language. It is also possible that a language can have less resemblance to its neighbours than to other, more remote languages, which is generally explained by a movement of the population. Romanian, for example, is closer to Italian and French than to Hungarian or the Slavic languages, because its bearers invaded a part of the former Roman Empire situated between Dacia and Italy. Hungarian is closer to Estonian and Finnish than to Romanian or Czech, because its bearers migrated to the northeastern part of Central Europe. It is probable, moreover, that a certain number of linguistic groups have disappeared without leaving any traces. Thus the IE languages that we know today are not necessarily all that existed. Finally, certain dialects are difficult to classify into well-determined families. This is notably the case with most of the IE dialects of northern Italy, such as Rhaetian (close to Illyrian, but which has also been influenced by Etruscan), Venetic (sometimes considered to be an Italic dialect, but which is closer to Greek than Italian), or Ligurian (intermediary between Italic and Celtic).

A quantitative analysis of the resemblances between the IE languages was undertaken in 1922 by the statistician JB Kruskal and the linguists Dyen and Blanck, who attempted to measure the frequency of terms of common origin in a certain number of languages, using a standard glottochronological list of 200 words. But they did not take into account the extinct languages, like Hittite and Tocharian, which reduces much of the value of their 'linguistic tree'. More recently, in 1995, two linguists and an information scientist from the University of Pennsylvania, Don Ringe, Ann Taylor, and Tandy Warnow, proposed a model based on a computer-simulated algorithm. This model confirms the great antiquity of the Anatolian group, but suggests that it evolved not from common IE, but from a language that no longer exists today but which is related to PIE. The Celtic and Italic languages would then be the next to separate from PIE, followed perhaps by Tocharian, then by Greek, Armenian, and Indo-Iranian. The Germanic languages would detach themselves from Balto-Slavic around the time that Greek emerged. They would then borrow largely from the Italic and Celtic languages. The Baltic and Slavic languages would be differentiated last. This is obviously only a hypothesis.

The idea that a linguistic continuum existed in Northern Europe from prehistoric times, hence prior to the ethnogenesis and glottogenesis of the Celtic, Germanic, Italic, Baltic, and Slavic languages, has already been advanced by Antoine Meillet in the course that he taught at the Collège de France in 1906–7.[171] On the basis of 38 lexical isoglosses, he put forward the notion of 'Northwest Indo-European', the common language from which the Germanic, Baltic, Slavic, and 'Italo-Celtic' languages would be derived. Some of these isoglosses have lost their demonstrative value today, but the general idea remains valid: a Northwestern IE linguistic community most certainly existed, and subsequently broke up into distinct

---

171   Cf. Antoine Meillet, *The Indo-European Dialects*.

linguistic unities.[172] Some authors connect Albanian to this group, and we can speculate whether or not to add Messapian. Wolfgang Meid deems that there are good reasons to believe that the 'Northwest group' also includes a language of which nothing remains for us, but whose existence explains certain linguistic facts better than recourse to a possible pre-IE substrate.[173] The isoglosses raised by Meillet do not, however, allow us to determine the genealogy of languages issued from the 'Northwest group'. In addition, aside from Indo-Iranian, Balto-Slavic, and perhaps Indo-Hittite, we no longer believe today in groups such as the 'Italo-Celtic', or even in a common ancestor of all the Italic languages. The 'Italo-Celtic' hypothesis was reexamined in 1917 by Alois Walde, who would divide this group into three sub-groups (Latin-Irish, Osco-Umbrian, and Britonnic). Meillet would reply in 1922 that this division 'clashes against the obvious unity of the Italic group on one hand, and of the Celtic group on the other'. In 1954, Walter Porzig attempted to show that the Italic languages occupied an intermediate position between the Celtic and Germanic languages. Today the 'Italo-Celtic' thesis only retains a few rare proponents.[174]

The existence of a Balto-Slavic group has also been contested. However, it seems more secure. The proximity of the Baltic and Slavic languages is almost equal to that of Indian and Iranian: in some respects, Proto-Slavic looks like a southern dialect of the Baltic group. But the lexical, grammatical, and morphological correspondences between the Balto-Slavic languages and the Germanic languages are equally important (around 43 per cent). The lexical correspondences above all feature the natural environment and parts of the body, and so on, while the common vocabulary relative to the more complex forms of social life are almost non-existent; this seems to suggest that the languages had a life in common prior to the metal ages, with an intervening separation occurring

---

172   Cf. Edgar C Polomé, 'The Indo-Europeanization of Northern Europe: The Linguistic Evidence', in *JIES*, Autumn–Winter 1990, pp. 331–338.

173   'Hans Kuhns "Nordwestblock" Hypothese', in *Anzeiger der Österreichischen Akademie der Wissenschaften*, 1984, pp. 2–21.

174   Bernard Sergent thinks that it is 'legitimate to speak of an Italo-Celtic language family divided into two large branches' (op. cit., p. 71).

very early on.[175] This extremely close proximity has been confirmed by the study of local hydronomy carried out by Jürgen Udolph.[176] In 1894, Karl Horst Schmidt also showed that the lexical correspondences between the Germanic and Balto-Slavic languages are extremely archaic, even in the religious domain.

In the past we have counted on the correspondences between Slavic and Iranian. Some have concluded that it is only after being separated from the Iranian group that the Slavic languages would have come closer to the Baltic languages, while the Germanic languages moved towards the Italic languages, and perhaps also Illyrian and Venetic. But these correspondences seem limited, and above all, they do not seem to go back beyond the relatively recent period which saw the Iranian group exert some influence on the Slavic world. In the Dnieper region situated between Ukraine and Belarus, linguists have identified more than thirty Iranian hydronyms (Udava, Uday, Artopolot, Ropsha, Svapa, etc.) probably dating from the Scythian cultures that developed in this region between the seventh and third centuries before our era.[177] Regarding the original homeland of the Proto-Slavs, authors are divided between the upper basin of the Vistula and the Oder (the western hypothesis), and those who place it southwest of their current habitat, in the middle basin of the Dneiper.

T Burrow[178] places the cradle of the Indo-Iranians in southern Russia, perhaps in the basin of the Volga, but does not have them initiate their migration before 2000. We know that the Indus civilisation began around 6500, and that it attained its apogee between 3100/2600 and 1900 with the cultures of Harappa and Mohenjo-Daro. In the most commonly held thesis, the collapse of the Harappan culture coincided with the arrival of the Indo-Aryans, doubtless from Bactria, upon the Indian subcontinent.

---

175 Cf. Christian Stang, *Lexikalische Sonderübereinstimmungen zwischen dem Slavischen, Baltischen und Germanischen* (Oslo: Universitetsforlaget, 1971).

176 *Die Stellung der Gewässernamen Polens innerhalb der alteuropäischen Hydronymie* (Heidelberg: Carl Winter, 1990).

177 Cf. D Ya Telegin, 'Iranian Hydronyms and Archaeological Cultures in the Eastern Ukraine', in *JIES*, Spring–Summer 1990, pp. 109–129.

178 *The Sanskrit Language* (London: Faber & Faber, 1955).

In the absence of archaeological traces of this penetration, all of these questions nevertheless remain controversial.[179]

The arrival in the Greek Peninsula of the Proto-Greeks, carrying dialects still identifiable to the Mycenaean period, is generally situated around 2300/2400 BCE, or the beginning of Early Helladic II. According to Marija Gimbutas, however, it would have begun between 2900 and

---

179 Asko Parpola, 'The Coming of the Aryans to Iran and India and the Cultural and Ethnic Identity of the Dasas', in *Studia Orientalia*, 1968, pp. 196–302, distinguishes two waves of migrations: those of the Aryans called 'Dasas' in the Vedas, bearers of the Iranian culture of the Bronze Age, which had penetrated into India from Baluchistan in the second millennium; and those, prior, of the Vedic Aryans, drinkers of *soma* and worshippers of Indra, coming from the Andronovo culture. On the chronological aspect of the debate, cf. DP Agrawal, RV Krishnamurthy, Sheela Kusumgar, and RK Pant, 'Chronology of Indian Prehistory from the Mesolithic Period to the Iron Age', in *Journal of Human Evolution*, January 1978, pp. 37–44. The uncertainties concerning the arrival of the Indo-Aryans in India are nourished today in this country by an entire series of 'anti-invasionist' theses, which hold that 'nothing attests to the existence of an Indo-Aryan or European invasion in the subcontinent of India at any time in prehistory or protohistory' (James R Schaffer, 'The Indo-Aryan Invasions: Cultural Myth and Archaeological Reality', in JR Lukacs (ed.), *The People of South Asia* (New York: Plenum Press, 1984, p. 88). The Vedic period corresponds to a simple internal restructuring of an indigenous culture resulting from the Indus civilisation which, in the same stroke, came to be considered as 'essentially Indo-Aryan' from the seventh millennium (Subhash C Kak, 'The Indus Tradition and the Indo-Aryans', in *JIES*, Spring 1992, p. 198). The original habitat of the Vedic Indians would be sought in the region of Sapta Saindhava, between the Ganges and the Indus, more specifically in the region surrounding the river Sarasvati (homonym of the wife of Brahma). It is the drying up of this sacred river, which happened around 1900 BCE, and not an exterior invasion, which caused the end of the Harappan culture. The authors who defend this radical thesis (David Frawley, SR Rao, Navaratna Rajaram, Subhak Kak, James R Schaffer, Mark Kenoyer, SP Gupta, Bhagwan Singh, BG Siddarth, KD Sethna, PV Pathak, KD Abhyankar, Shrikant Talageri, S Kalyanaraman, etc.) also affirm that no material proof exists for an arrival in India of Dravidian populations which replaced the previous aboriginal population, and go so far as to call that the theme of a IE invasion a 'Eurocentric colonialist myth of the twentieth century', destined to mask the fact that Vedic India is 'the oldest, greatest, and most significant of all the cultures in the world' (David Frawley, *The Myth of the Aryan Invasion of India* [New Delhi: Voice of India, 1994], p. 54). This thesis of the autochthony of the Dravidian civilisation and the Indo-Aryan civilisation, which represents so many successive phases of one and the same local culture, is in obvious contradiction to all the data of linguistics and of comparative mythology. It seems inspired above all by an exacerbated Indian nationalism. An identical reticence or reserve regarding the fact of IE are sometimes encountered in Greece, and indeed in the Celtic world.

2600. This ingress could only have taken place from the north.[180] Whereas Gimbutas has the Proto-Greeks arrive from the culture of Baden-Vučedol in the northwest of Yugoslavia, János Makkay places their origin at the end of the middle Copper Age among the Bodrogkeresztùr-Salcuta culture from the southern section of the Hungarian plain and the lower course of the Danube. Albania, Macedonia, and perhaps Thessaly would have been Indo-Europeanised by the end of the Neolithic, and Boeotia from the beginning of the third millennium. Following this, the movement would reach Peloponnesus and Attica around 2300 BCE, before spreading around the Aegean islands and the coasts of Asia Minor, where the differentiation of the Greek dialects would be completed.[181] The new culture would stabilise itself during the Mycenaean period, between 1600 and 1200 BCE. The exact origin of the Mycenaeans has always been an object of debate.[182] The Dorians (whose name could be close to that of the Thuringians) only emerge around 1200 BCE, perhaps in the context of the vast movement of people through which the 'People of the North Sea' appeared in the Middle East. Their linguistic system presents traits more archaic than those of the first Achaeans. For André Martinet, 'that the ancestors of the Achaeans and those of the Dorians belonged, in the third millennium, to the same branch of the Indo-European family, is not established'.[183]

The affinities of Greek and Armenian have been noted by Holger Pedersen from 1925. Numerous works have since suggested that Proto-

180 Cf. Michel B Sakellariou, *Les Proto-Grecs* (Athens: Ekdotikè Athenon, 1980); H Arthur Bankoff & Frederick A Winter, 'Northern Intruders in LH IIIC Greece: A View from the North', in *JIES*, Spring–Summer 1984, pp. 1–30; and Stephan Hiller, 'Die Ethnogenese der Griechen aus der Sicht der Vor- und Frühgeschichte', in Wolfram Bernhard & Anneliese Kandler-Pálsson (eds.), *Ethnogenese europäischer Völker aus der Sicht der Anthropologie und Vor- und Frühgeschichte* (Stuttgart: Gustav Fischer, 1986), pp. 21–37.

181 Cf. John Chadwick, 'The Prehistory of the Greek Language', in *The Cambridge Ancient History*, vol. 2 (Cambridge: Cambridge University Press, 1963), p. 15.

182 Cf. Alexander Häusler, 'Die Indoeuropäisierung Griechenlands nach Aussage der Grab- und Bestattungssitten', in *Slovenska Archeologia*, 1981, pp. 59–66; and Robert Drews, *The Coming of the Greeks* (Princeton: Princeton University Press, 1988).

183 'Les Indo-Européens et la Grèce', in *Diogène*, January–March 1989, p. 12.

Greek and Proto-Armenian only formed a single language in the third millennium, and that the overestimation of the opposition between *centum* languages (such as Greek) and *satem* languages (such as Armenian) have prevented us from knowing this earlier. The phonological parallelism of the two languages is well-established today. Lexical correspondences, which are numerous, have been chiefly studied by Georg Renatus Solta.[184] In certain respects, Armenian appears as a kind of bridge between Greek and Indo-Iranian.

On the basis of linguistic achievements of the last decades, Wolfgang Meid suggested dividing PIE into three distinct periods.[185] Stage I (*frühindogermanisch*)[186] corresponds to the primitive state of the language, before the fifth millennium, upon which we can only speculate; Stage II (*mittelindogermanisch*)[187] corresponds to the last common stage (fifth and fourth millennia), during which Hittite and the other Anatolian languages separated from PIE; Stage III (*spätindogermanisch*)[188] corresponds to the time when the two principal groups — the Southeast and Northwest — were already separated. Despite the criticism to which it has been subjected,[189] this model adapts itself perfectly 'to the schema that we can propose for the dispersion of Indo-European peoples from historical and archaeological records'.[190] We can also see that the different stages correspond to evolution in the domains of social organisation and religion.

---

184 *Die Stellung des Armenischen im Kreise der indogermanischen Sprachen* (Vienna: Mechitharisten, 1960).

185 'Probleme der räumlichen und zeitlichen Gliederung des Indogermanischen', in Helmut Rix (ed.), *Flexion und Wortbildung*, op. cit., pp. 204–219; and 'The Temporal and Spatial Patterning of Indo-European', in *NOWELE*, 1983, pp. 3–21. Cf. also Erich Neu, 'Zur Rekonstruktion des indogermanischen Verbalsystems', in Anna Morpurgo Davies & Wolfgang Meid (eds.), *Studies in Greek, Italic, and Indo-European Linguistics*, op. cit., pp. 239 ff.

186 Early Indo-Germanic. — Tr.

187 Middle Indo-Germanic. — Tr.

188 Late Indo-Germanic. — Tr.

189 Cf. Bernfried Schlerath, 'Sprachvergleich und Rekonstruktion: Methoden und Möglichkeiten', in *Incontri linguistici*, 1982–83, pp. 53–69; and 'On the Reality and Status of a Reconstructed Language', in *JIES*, Spring–Summer 1987, pp. 41–46.

190 Bernard Sergent, op. cit., p. 152.

A model closely approaching this was proposed by Francisco Rodriguez Adrados.[191] According to Adrados, Stage I of common IE (for which he reserves the term PIE) corresponded to a non-inflected phase of the language. This would have been monosyllabic, if not monovocalic. Deprived of morphology, properly speaking, it possessed a developed consonantal system, but a rudimentary system of vowels. This pre-inflectional stage would have been succeeded by the first inflected, monothematic stage. This is Stage II, corresponding to the *mittelindogermanisch* of Meid, which was connected to the Anatolian group, among which monothematic inflection is preserved. Stage III, or the 'Brugmannian' stage, is characterised by the appearance of polythematic inflection, including the distinction between masculine and feminine adjectives, of degrees of comparison within the adjective, and of differentiation of tenses and modes within the verbal system, and so on. This evolution was principally expressed in India and Greece (stage IIIA), whereas in the Northwest languages, some of these developments were not known (stage IIIB).

The Contributions of Anthropology

In 1855, Karl Vogt seems to have been the first to speak of the 'Indo-European race'. He was rapidly followed by numerous authors, such as Adolphe Pictet or the historian Jacob Kruger who, in 1885, did not hesitate to assimilate the IE to the descendants of the 'giant' Enak (Anak) mentioned in the Bible (Numbers 13:33)! This unreasonable reinterpretation of the facts of culture and language in terms of 'race', as if the three notions were interchangeable, would succumb to its own destiny, as we know. Otto Bremer from 1900 and Otto Schrader from 1901 have nevertheless cautioned against this approach. Previously, Friedrich Max Müller, having himself formulated and popularised a number of racial classifications

---

191 *Die räumliche und sprachliche Differenzierung des Indoeuropäischen im Lichte der Vor- und Frühgeschichte* (Innsbruck: Institut der Sprachwissenschaft der Universität, 1982); and 'Ideas on the Typology of Proto-Indo-European', in *JIES*, Spring–Summer 1987, pp. 97–119.

since 1849, also stressed that 'speaking of the Aryan race is as ludicrous as speaking of an dolichocephalic dictionary'.[192] The idea of the 'Indo-European race' (or 'Aryan') is in fact meaningless, as is the idea of wanting to seek the IE origins of the White race. The principle reason is not the absence of automatic correlation between *ethnos* and language,[193] for it is not forbidden to think, in the case of PIE, that the conditions of isolation necessary for the formation of a unitary language could have also favoured the ethnogenesis of a rather homogenous population, anthropologically speaking. Rather, it is the fact that since the beginning of the Upper Palaeolithic, around 40,000/30,000 BCE, which coincides with the end of the Mousterian in Western Europe, the flowering of the Aurignacian culture, and the appearance of the first types of Cro-Magnon, all the identifiable skeletons in Europe are clearly of the Europid[194] type. There is thus no place to think that the IE populations belonged to a 'race' different to that of the pre-IE populations — or to that of people who still make use of non-IE languages today (Basque, Finnish, Hungarian). We also recall that the interpretation in terms of 'races' of three 'colours' (Old Indian *varṇa-*, Avestan *pishtra-*), which have given their names to the great Indian castes, an explanation that we still find at the end of the 1950s in the work of DM Majumdar,[195] is also abandoned today. The three 'colours' do not refer to anthropological facts, but to a very ancient symbolism (white, red, and yellow in India, or blue-black in Iran) which issued from the cosmology of 'three heavens'.

It should not be forgotten, too, that the historical IE cultures are from mixed societies, born from the fusion of an IE element which did not necessarily maintain the dominant position, and a pre-IE substrate of vary-

---

192 *The Biographies of Words and the Home of the Aryas* (London: Longmans Green, 1888).

193 Cf. on this subject Karl J Narr, *Kulturelle Vereinheitlichung und sprachliche Zersplitterung: Ein Beispiel aus dem Südwesten der Vereinigten Staaten* (Opladen: Westdeutscher, 1985).

194 Caucasian. — Tr.

195 *Races and Cultures of India* (Bombay: Asia Publishing House, 1958). Cf. also I Karve, *Hindu Society: An Interpretation* (Poona: Deshmukh & Co., 1961).

ing importance, of which we know very little; that is to say, a mixture of populations involving different human types present in Europe since the Upper Palaeolithic. This mixture could be translated by the phenomena of syncretism or symbiosis into the domains of language, technology, beliefs, social organisation, and so forth. Bernard Sergent speaks in this regard of an 'ethnic synthesis, at least between the local prehistoric populations, i.e., those whose roots among other populations in the area go back to Palaeolithic times, and of immigrants bearing an IE language whose imposition upon the territory, along with local evolution, leads to the historically attested languages'.[196] In this sense, as Herman Hirt has already noted, it is not incorrect to say that 'all the known Indo-European peoples have been Indo-Europeanised',[197] since it is from an external influx that they draw their IE character. Christian J Guyonvarc'h and François Le Roux, who recall that 'Europe evaluates itself not by race but by language and ethnicity', emphasise for their part that 'save for rare exceptions, we have no means to distinguish what will eventually be of pure origin and what will be non-Indo-European, that is to say, the result of a previous assimilation, from an ancient Indo-European ethnicity characterised by language and religion'.[198] 'It is precisely because it is unverifiable', they add, 'that the racial criteria is frequently adduced in the contemporary Indo-European domain to the benefit of ideologies which have no Indo-European basis'.[199]

It is nonetheless true, as with any other human population, that the members of the original IE community present bioanthropological characteristics which are obviously not forbidden to research. One of these characteristics is a fair complexion (red or blond hair, blue eyes) that numerous authors have attributed to them, whether based upon ancient descriptions and testimonies, or by analogy with the physical charac-

---

196 Op. cit., p. 18.
197 Ibid.
198 *La civilisation celtique*, op. cit., pp. 23 & 85.
199 Ibid., p. 22.

teristics of contemporary people who occupy territories that the home-land might have been situated within. In the middle of the nineteenth century, the Belgian naturalist Omalius d'Halloy already affirmed that 'the Aryan languages were incarnated in the blond type', an affirmation echoed by Matthäus Much, Theodor Poesch, Otto Hauser, etc. In 1878, Poesche went so far as to imagine that the original IE homeland was situated in the marshlands of Pripet, because we encounter there, he assures us, a significant number of albinos (the albino type being falsely equated with a supreme-blond type)![200] Other authors incorrectly conclude that Indo-Europeanness was identical to blondness. However, as Isaac Taylor already emphasised,[201] if there is a population among which the blond type predominates, it is clearly among the Finns and Estonians, whose language is strictly non-IE, since it belongs to the Finno-Ugric language family. Although the blond type could have been dominant among the IE, it does not necessarily follow that this trait has always belonged to them exclusively. The existence of a blond type among them can, however, elucidate the question of the homeland.

Bernard Sergent explains the blondness attributed to a number of IE deities and heroes as a 'symbolic coding', and rejects the idea that we can extend the argument to a conclusion about the actual blondness of the PIE peoples. In the case of mythological personages (for example the IE god Indra, entitled *hari-kesa*, 'blond hair' in the *Rig Veda*, or further, in Homer, Achilles, Odysseus, Meleagre, Menelaus, Rhadamanthus, etc.), this explanation could possibly be accepted. There is no doubt that blond has a symbolic value, as testified by the number of popular traditions that attribute a negative value to brown hair. It remains, however, to examine the origin of this 'coding', and to ask whether the valorisation of blondness had been developed among predominantly brown-haired populations.

---

200 Theodor Poesche, *Die Arier: Ein Beitrag zur historischen Anthropologie*, Hermann Costenoble, Jena 1878. Cf. James P Mallory, 'Human Populations and the Indo-European Problem', in *JIES*, Winter 1991–92, pp. 131–154.

201 *The Origin of the Aryans: An Account of the Prehistoric Ethnology and Civilization of Europe* (London: Walter Scott & New York: Gumboldt Publishers, 1890).

But the explanation no longer matters when we have the testimonies of the populations themselves. These attestations are not only numerous, they also agree. Egyptian texts describe the 'Libyan' tribes linked to the 'Sea Peoples from the North' who invaded Egypt in 1227 BCE, as blond haired and blue eyed. In Chinese texts from the second century BCE, we find similar descriptions for the Tocharian populations, descriptions confirmed today by the discovery of 'mummies' with blond or red hair from the Tarim basin. Herodotus attributes blue eyes to the Scythians. The Greek geographer Posidonius of Rhodes described the Germans as an essentially blond people, which confirms Tacitus (*De Germania*, 4). Other Classical authors also describe the Celts, the Geto-Dacians, and the Thracians as people with blond hair and blue eyes. Of the 747 mythic or historical personages whose physical appearance is described in the ancient sources (350 among the Greeks and 111 among the Romans), the palaeographer Wilhelm Sieglin, who was one of the 'discoverers' of Tocharian in 1908, found 586 blonds (including Alexander the Great, Alcibiades, Anacreon, Apollonius of Tyre, Denis of Syracuse, Critias, Cato the Elder, Pompey, Sulla, Anthony, Augustus, Domitian, Trajan, Commodus, Caracalla, etc.) and 151 with brown hair.[202]

The adaptive value of human pigmentation is today well established: the closer a population is to the equator, the darker its pigmentation; the further away they are, the more their pigmentation is fair.[203] Dark skin offers better protection against ultraviolet rays, which can be fatal among children and causes skin cancer in adults. This is why populations from tropical regions developed darker pigmentation of the skin, eyes, and hair, as well as weight reduction, nose size, and thicker skin layers to protect against the carcinogenic effects of ultraviolet. Light pigmentation, on the other hand, has a selective value in cold or temperate regions, favouring

---

202 Wilhelm Sieglin, *Die blonden Haaren der indogermanischen Völker des Altertums: Eine Sammlung der antiken Zeugnisse als Beitrag zur Indogermanenfrage* (Munich: JF Lehmanns, 1935). Whereas the Classical Greek authors frequently attributed blond hair to their characters, we note, however, that the individuals represented on their painted pots and vases are almost always brown-haired.

203 Cf. AM Brues, 'Rethinking Human Pigmentation', in *American Journal of Physical Anthropology*, 1975, pp. 387–392.

the synthesis of vitamin D, whose deficiency causes rickets.[204] It has also been shown, from the correlation of eye and hair colour among spouses, that these traits influence the choice of sexual partners, which obviously has an impact on genetic pools.[205] Even today, it is in Scandinavia and the Baltic countries that we find the highest degree of blondness (54–76 per cent on the eastern coast of the Baltic), with an almost homozygous blue eye phenotype (> 95 per cent in Sweden, 85–98 per cent in the Peribaltic regions). The appearance of blond hair most likely accompanies the phenomenon of depigmentation that occurred in the Palaeolithic during the last glaciation period in the circumpolar regions of central and eastern Northern Europe. In the nineteenth century, Thomas Huxley[206] already believed that the phenomenon was produced in a zone running from the Baltic to the Urals. Lothar Kilian,[207] who emphasised the presence of a blond element among the PIE, summarised that this element belonged to two different types, Nordic and Dalic. The Nordic type is as blond as the Dalic, but its skeleton is like the Mediterranean type, such that we can consider it like a depigmented Mediterranean. The distribution of blood groups shows that this type, for whom the B group is rare, is not formed in Asia, where it is by contrast frequent. The Nordic and Dalic types result from depigmentation, occurring during the Würm glaciation, from the Brünn and Combe Capelle types on one hand, and Cro-Magnon on the other. Kilian concludes that it would be arbitrary to attribute a single Nordic type to the Indo-European peoples. 'By reason of the proximity

---

204 Cf. WF Loomis, 'Skin-Pigmented Regulation of Vitamin-B Biosynthese', in *Science*, 1967, pp. 501–506; RM Neer, 'The Evolutionary Significance of Vitamin D, Skin Pigment and Ultraviolet Light', in *American Journal of Physical Anthropology*, 1975, pp. 409–416.

205 Cf. Widukind Lenz, *Medical Genetics* (Chicago: University of Chicago Press, 1963); G Bräuer & VP Chopra, 'Schätzungen der Heritabilität von Haar- und Augenfarbe', in *Anthropologische Anzeiger*, 1978, pp. 109–120.

206 'The Aryan Question and Pre-Historic Man', in *The Nineteenth Century*, 1890, pp. 750–765. [Thomas Huxley (1825–1895) was an English biologist who was one of the first and most prominent champions of Darwin's theory of evolution, and was the grandfather of Aldous Huxley. — Ed.]

207 *Zum Ursprung der Indogermanen: Forschungen aus Linguistik, Prähistorie und Anthropologie* (Bonn: Rudolf Habelt, 1983).

of the Nordics and the Dalics, as from their partial liaison', he writes, 'the original IE people should bear a Dalic component, of unequal significance depending on location. The other components, in particular the Mediterranean, are not to be excluded.'[208]

If we admit that the bearers of PIE came from a (primary or secondary) homeland situated in Northern Europe, the presence of a blond element is perfectly ordinary. It is the complete opposite that would be surprising. This presence is, on the contrary, more difficult to explain if we reach for a homeland situated in Asia Minor or in the Mediterranean region. IM Diakonov used this argument against the theses of Gamkrelidze and Ivanov: if Indo-Europeanisation was due to the arrival in Europe of a population originally form the Near East, and if it is given that dark eye colour formed a dominant characteristic (and blue eyes a recessive characteristic), the population of Northern Europe could not have the fair complexion that still belongs to it today: 'A population that has a blue-eyed majority cannot have a population that has a dark-eyed majority for its ancestors.'[209] The same argument has been repeated by Raymond V Sidrys,[210] who feels that the almost homozygotic character of the blue-eye phenotype in Northern Europe refutes all the theories that attribute the Indo-Europeanisation of Europe to a population that came from Armenia or Anatolia.

In the nineteenth century, researchers also clashed over the question of whether the IE were brachycephalic or dolichocephalic. This war lost its relevance when it was noted that the skeletons of the Nordic and the Mediterranean type were practically identical (except for the size of orbit); the two types are only differentiated by their soft parts, and furthermore, the dolichocephalic type is far from being the only one to characterise them. From 1883, Rudolf Virchow could affirm that the craniological

---

208 Ibid., pp. 152–153.

209 'On the Origin of Speakers of Indo-European', in *JIES*, Spring–Summer 1985, p. 153.

210 'The Light Eye and Hair Cline: Implications for Indo-European Migrations to Northern Europe', in Karlene Jones-Bley & Martin E Huld (eds.), *The Indo-Europeanization of Northern Europe*, op. cit., pp. 330–349.

type of the IE included as many dolichocephalics as meso- and brachy-cephalics. Since the 1960s, the renovation of physical anthropological methods (development of osteometric techniques, systematic recourse to information technology, etc.) has allowed skeletons to be studied better. We know today that at the beginning of the Neolithic, two principal types were represented in Europe: on one hand a 'western' type of Mediterranean origin, dolichocephalic or mesocephalic, and more or less slender (leptomorphic), of medium or large size; on the other hand, an 'eastern' type, larger (hypermorphic), mesocephalic or brachycephalic, sometimes called 'Cro-Magnid' or 'Proto-Europid C'. The two types are well represented, but in varying proportions, on sites corresponding to cultures recognised as IE, without which it will always be possible to relate them to IE properly speaking, or to an eventual pre-IE substrate. The slender type is more frequent in the Corded Ware culture. The robust type subdivides itself into a subgroup of the accentuated type, well-represented in the Dnieper-Donetz culture, and a subgroup of the attenuated type: mesocephalic, mesomorphic, wide-faced, low orbits, above all present in the Kurgan culture.[211]

More recently, the study of genetic markers comparable to that of languages has given birth to a new discipline: ethnogenetics. It bases itself on the observation that the speakers of different languages in Europe are genetically different from each other. The fact of speaking the same language effectively favours a relative endogamy, and thus a concentration of genetic pools, such that 'it is legitimate to expect a basic similarity between biological evolution and linguistic evolution'.[212] 'Isolation, which

---

211 Cf. Olga Necrasov, 'Physical Anthropological Characteristics of Skeletons from the Kurgan Graves of Romania', in *JIES*, Autumn–Winter 1980, pp. 337–343; Ilse Schwidetzky & FW Rösing, 'The Influence of the Steppe People Based on Physical Anthropological Data in Special Consideration to the Corded-Battle-Axe Culture', ibid., pp. 345–360; and Roland Menk, 'A Synopsis of the Physical Anthropology of the Corded Ware Complex on the Background of the Expansion of the Kurgan Culture', ibid., pp. 361–392. The type of the Kurgan culture has been chiefly studied by Russian and Ukrainian anthropologists (TC Konduktorova, SI Kruts, GP Zinevich).

212 Luca L Cavalli-Sforza, *Genes, Peoples, and Languages*, op. cit., p. 150. Cf. also G Barbujani & RR Sokal, 'Zones of Sharp Genetic Change in Europe are also Linguistic

could result from geographic, ecological, or social barriers', writes Luca L Cavalli-Sforza:

> reduces the likelihood of marriages between populations, and as a result, recip-
> rocally isolated populations will evolve independently and gradually become
> different. Genetic differentiation of reciprocally isolated populations occurs
> slowly but regularly over time. We can expect the same thing to happen with
> languages: isolation diminishes cultural exchange, and the two languages will
> drift apart. Even if glottochronological estimates of the time of separation are
> not always as exact as we would like, in general languages do diverge increas-
> ingly with time. In principle, therefore, the linguistic tree and the genetic tree of
> human populations should agree, since they reflect the same history of popula-
> tions splitting and evolving independently.[213]

Researches have been undertaken, notably by Cavalli-Sforza, Alberto Piazza, and Paolo Menozzi in Italy, and by Robert Sokal in the United States, to try to determine correlations between the regional genetic frequencies in Europe and the data of linguistics or archaeology.[214] Some specimens allow us to establish the relative frequency of 95 alleles collected from the living populations in some 3,000 different locations. The most striking result is the remarkable stability or homogeneity of the genomic structures of most of the ethnic groups in Europe. Ethnogenetics has also allowed us to note that the linguistic border separating the IE languages

---

Boundaries', in *Proceedings of the National Academy of Sciences*, 1990, pp. 1816–1819.

213 *Genes, Peoples, and Languages*, op. cit., pp. 150–151.

214 Cf. RR Sokal, 'Genetic, Geographic and Linguistic Distances in Europe', in *Proceedings of the National Academy of Sciences*, 1988, pp. 1722–1726; Luca L Cavalli-Sforza, 'Genes, Peoples and Languages', in *Scientific American*, 1991, pp. 104–110; and Luca L Cavalli-Sforza & Alberto Piazza, 'Human Genomic Diversity in Europe: A Summary of Recent Research and Prospects for the Future', in *European Journal of Human Genetics*, 1993, pp. 3–18. Cf. also Luca L Cavalli-Sforza, Alberto Piazza, Paolo Menozzi, & JL Mountain, 'Reconstruction of Human Evolution: Bringing Together Genetic, Archaeological and Linguistic Data', in *Proceedings of the National Academy of Sciences*, 1988, pp. 8002–8006; Luca L Cavalli-Sforza et al., *The History and Geography of Human Genes* (Princeton: Princeton University Press, 1994); Luca L Cavalli-Sforza, 'An Evolutionary View of Linguistics', in MY Chen & OJL Tzeng (eds.), *In Honour of William S. Y. Yang* (Taipei: Pyramid Press, 1994); and Alberto Piazza, R Sabina, E Minch, Paolo Menozzi, JL Mountain, & Luca L Cavalli-Sforza, 'Genetics and the Origin of European Languages', in *Proceeding of the National Academy of Sciences*, 1995, pp. 5836–5840.

from the Finno-Ugric languages also corresponds to a genetic border.[215] Other studies have been made on the genetic markers of the population of the Indian subcontinent.[216] These have revealed a greater genetic heterogeneity than we expected from the endogamy implied by the caste system, including in the Brahman caste, notably Maharashtra. The greatest genetic homogeneity (32.4 per cent variation) has been observed in the northwest, which is the area which received the most invasions.

The method used by ethnogenetics has been debated, however, for it only takes into account current linguistic borders. These are not necessarily identical to those which existed in the past. In addition, ethnogenetics is incapable of furnishing an absolute chronology for the formation of the genetic pools that it studies, for apparently the tick of the molecular clock is as completely subject to variations as the rhythm of linguistic evolution. Cavalli-Sforza and Piazza thus affirm that 'the main ingredient in the European genetic landscape consists of a gradient that gradually extends to the northwest from the Near East'.[217] Colin Renfrew has based himself on this observation in order to develop his thesis of an Indo-Europeanisation of Europe from Anatolia. Strictly speaking, Cavalli-Sforza and his collaborators have not demonstrated anything as such, however, because the genetic frequencies that they have used as evidence can just as well refer to the movements of populations before the IE migrations.[218] At first glance, the results which they have attained are quite congruent with the idea of a migration of Neolithic Anatolian farmers introducing agriculture into

---

215 Cf. CR Guglielmino-Matessi, Alberto Piazza, Paolo Menozzi, & Luca L Cavalli-Sforza, 'Uralic Genes in Europe', in *American Journal of Physical Anthropology*, 1990, pp. 57–68. On the previous state of research: Karin Mark, *Zur Herkunft der finnisch-ugrischen Völker vom Standpunkt der Anthropologie* (Tallinn: Eesti Raamat, 1970).

216 Cf. KC Malhotra, 'Morphological Composition of the People of India', in *Journal of Human Evolution*, January 1978, pp. 45–53; LD Sanghvi, 'Nature of Genetic Variation in the People of Western India', ibid., pp. 55–65; and V Balakrishnan, 'A Preliminary Study of the Genetic Distances among Some Populations of the Indian Sub-Continent', ibid., pp. 67–75.

217 'Human Genomic Diversity in Europe', art. cit., p. 283.

218 Cf. James P Mallory, 'Human Populations and the Indo-European Problem', art. cit., pp. 144–148.

Europe from the seventh millennium,[219] a migration for which there is no reason to think that it was synonymous with Indo-Europeanisation. However, there does not exist for this epoch any archaeological trace of a grand-scale migration, neither from Anatolia to the Aegean Sea and then towards Europe, nor from the southeast of the European continent towards the northwest.[220] Since the Neolithic era, the Aegean Sea was a simple area of exchange and contact. If a migration of such magnitude happened, it is unclear why it would only be directed towards the northwest, and not also towards the northeast. All the data at our disposal concerning Eastern Europe attests that the migrations which have taken place happened in the opposite direction, that is, from the northeast towards the south. It is therefore permissible to ask if the gradient indicated by Cavalli-Sforza and Piazza does not refer to a still earlier period than that of the diffusion of agriculture, in other words at a time where a population of hunter-gatherers came from the Near East to spread the modern human type across the whole European continent. Another study to test different hypotheses concerning the homeland of the IE[221] has resulted in a stalemate: no significant correlation could have been found between the distribution of languages, genetic frequencies, and the patterns proposed in these theories.

---

219 Cf. Albert J Ammerman & Luca L Cavalli-Sforza, 'Measuring the Rate of Spread of Early Farming in Europe', in *Man*, 1971, pp. 674–688; Paolo Menozzi, Alberto Piazza, & Luca L Cavalli-Sforza, 'Synthetic Maps of Human Gene Frequencies in Europeans', in *Science*, 1 September 1978, pp. 786–792; 'The Wave of Advance Model for the Spread of Agriculture in Europe', in Colin Renfrew, KL Cooke et al., *Transformations, Mathematical Approaches to Culture Change* (New York: Academic Press, 1979), pp. 275–294; and *The Neolithic Transition and the Genetics of Populations in Europe* (Princeton: Princeton University Press, 1984); and RR Sokal, NL Oden, & C Wilson, 'Genetic Evidence for the Spread of Agriculture in Europe by Demic Diffusion', in *Nature*, 1991, pp. 143–145.

220 Cf. Harald Haarman, 'Contact Linguistics, Archaeology and Ethnogenetics: An Interdisciplinary Approach to the Indo-European Homeland Problem', in *JIES*, Autumn–Winter 1994, p. 283.

221 RR Sokal, NL Oden, & BA Thomson, 'Origins of the Indo-Europeans: Genetic Evidence', in *Proceedings of the National Academy of Sciences*, 1992, pp. 7669–7673.

The Thesis of Colin Renfrew

All hypotheses concerning the original homeland must be compatible with the data of a linguistic, archaeological, and anthropological nature that we have enumerated. The homeland must be situated in a location compatible with our knowledge of the geographic distribution and the evolution of IE languages, in which the natural, cultural, and human environment corresponds to the reconstructed IE lexicon. Its identification must also take into account the emphasis of migrations, in the period 4500/2500 BCE, corresponding to what we know of the diffusion of language and PIE culture. Few hypotheses advanced to this day satisfy all these requirements. Localities such as the Semitic and Mediterranean countries, Arabia, Syria, Africa, but also Western Europe, have been abandoned today. A wide enough consensus places the original homeland in Europe, or in the immediate proximity of Europe, but within this vast territory, the proposed solutions are numerous.

Five major theses remain present: (1) the Anatolian thesis of the seventh millennium (Renfrew, 1987); (2) the Anatolian thesis of the fourth and fifth millennia (Gamkrelidze and Ivanov, 1985); (3) the Balkano-Danubian thesis (Diakonov, 1985); (4) the Nordic-Pontic thesis (Gimbutas, 1966); and (5) the Northern European thesis (Kilian, 1983). These are the theories which we will now examine.

The thesis of Colin Renfrew[222] is able to be summarised simply. The diffusion of IE languages would be indistinguishable from the progressive introduction into Europe, from an original homeland situated in central Anatolia (present-day Turkey) of a new system of production characterised by the cultivation of wheat and barley, the raising of sheep and goats, cows, oxen, and pigs. The PIE are thus none other than the first Neolithic farmers who, from the seventh millennium, introduced a new way of life to the Mesolithic European populations, according to a process that Renfrew

---

222 *Archaeology and Language: The Puzzle of Indo-European Origins* (London: Jonathan Cape, 1987); and 'The Origins of Indo-European Languages', in *Scientific American*, October 1989, pp. 106–114.

compares to the diffusion of the Bantu languages in South Africa, which was originally populated by Khoisan hunter-gatherers. The model rests on the idea that agriculture increases population density in the areas in which it is introduced, such that part of the populace finds itself obligated to emigrate, resulting in the proliferation of a new mode of life over greater and greater distances. The progression of the PIE proto-language and its ensuing differentiation is therefore explained by the cultivation of new land by successive generations and by the superiority of the new mode of production over the former. Supposing 'an interval between generations of 25 years', and that 'on coming of age each farmer moves 18 kilometers (in a random direction) from the parental homestead to establish his own farm', Renfrew concludes that agriculture had 'spread across Europe as a wave progressing at an average velocity of one kilometer per year. At that pace it would have taken about 1,500 years for the farming economy to reach northern Europe'.[223]

From the Anatolian homeland, which Renfrew places in a region situated between Çatul Hüyük and Çayönü, agriculture, and with it Indo-Europeanisation, successively reached the islands of the Aegean Sea, Greece, and India, then the Balkans and the basin of the Danube, Central Europe, and Italy, and finally Northern and Western Europe through to the Atlantic Coast, Great Britain, Ireland, and Scandinavia. Having arrived in Greece by the second half of the seventh millennium, the IE reached the north and west of the Alps around 4000, before reaching the Orkney Islands in the north of Scotland around 3500.

The IE therefore have a completely different character than that which we commonly attribute to them. Rejecting all theories of invasion or conquest by pastoral, mounted, warrior peoples, Renfrew assumes simple 'waves of advance' (or 'waves of propogation')—a model which he borrows from the works of Luca L Cavalli-Sforza and Albert J Ammermann — which would have been the acts of peaceful farmers: 'My hypothesis also implies that the first Indo-European speakers were not

---

223 'The Origins of Indo-European Languages', art. cit., p. 111.

invading warriors with a centrally organized society but peasant farmers whose societies were basically egalitarian and who in the course of an entire lifetime moved perhaps only a few kilometers.'[224] This thesis is not new. It recommences by extending the thesis of Pedro Bosch-Gimpera, who assimilates the IE to Danubian farmers of the fifth millennium, and also overlaps with that of F Flor.[225] Although it is not cited, it also corresponds to the hypothesis put forward in the 1940s by Pia Laviosa-Zambotta regarding the diffusion of agriculture in Europe.[226] To sustain this, Colin Renfrew unfortunately sees himself obliged to reject almost all of the conclusions to which IE studies have come for more than a century. Dismissing Benveniste and Dumézil in a few paragraphs, he denies any validity to the comparative history of religions, denounces the 'decoy of the proto-lexicon', and tends to discredit all the reconstructive efforts of linguistic palaeontology. He rejects everything that we know of PIE social organisation and of the IE system of kinship. He almost completely neglects the question of substrata, adstrata, and superstrata. Dismissing any reference to the Baltic group, he forms inaccurate assumptions about the origin of the Celts and the prehistoric development of the Greeks. We understand that the vast majority of specialists have refused to follow him, delivering the severest of criticisms.[227]

---

224 Ibid., p. 113.

225 'Die Indogermanen in der Völkerkunde', in Helmut Arntz (ed.), *Germanen und Indogermanen*, op. cit., vol. 1, pp. 69–129.

226 *Le più antiche civiltà nordiche e il problema degli Ugro-Finni et degli Indoeuropee* (Milan: Principato, 1941); *Le più antiche culture agricole europee* (Milan: Principato, 1943); *La successione delle gravitazioni indo-europee verso il Mediterraneo e la genesi della civiltà europea* (Firenze 1950); and *España e Italia ante de Romanos* (Madrid 1955).

227 These critiques have come from all sides. Cf. notably Wolfgang Meid, *Archäologie und Wissenschaft*, op. cit.; Jan Best, 'Comparative Indo-European Linguistics and Archaeology: Towards a Historical Integration', in *JIES*, Autumn–Winter 1989, pp. 335–340; Mark R Stefanovich, 'Can Archaeology and Historical Linguistics Coexist? A Critical Review of Colin Renfrew's *Archaeology and Language: The Puzzle of Indo-European Origins*', in *The Mankind Quarterly*, Autumn–Winter 1989, pp. 129–158; Michael Everson, 'Picture Out of Focus: Colin Renfrew's *Archaeology and Language: The Puzzle of Indo-European Origins*', ibid., pp. 159–173; Ralph M Rowlett, 'Research Directions in Early Indo-European Archaeology', in *History of Religions*, May 1990,

The objections that we can address to Colin Renfrew are in fact of many kinds. First, the thesis rests on the following syllogism: (1) agriculture is diffused very early in Europe from the Near East; (2) the diffusion of IE languages cannot be attributed to invasions that occurred later; and (3) it follows that the Indo-Europeans are indistinguishable from the first farmers, and that the IE languages are only, to varying degrees, Anatolian transformed by 'Creolisation'. The first premise is not necessarily very precise, the second is entirely false, and so too is the conclusion.

We generally place the birth of agriculture in the ninth millennium, in the 'fertile crescent', which extends from Mesopotamia to southern Palestine, passing through the southeast of Turkey, Syria, and Lebanon. Its bearers would then have penetrated the European continent, where they could have given birth to the cultures that Marija Gimbutas gathered together under the name of 'Old Europe'. Agriculture appears in Greece around 5000 BCE. It reaches the Netherlands a millennium later. However, this pattern, as we have said, is not always confirmed by archaeology. It is explicitly rejected by authors such as Roben Dennel[228] or Graeme Barker[229] who, basing themselves on the example of the British Isles, believe that agriculture resulted in Europe from autochthonous, parallel developments. In this context, the system of 'Old Europe' owes nothing to the first farmers, but goes back to the Upper European Palaeolithic.

---

pp. 415–418; Jean Haudry, 'Débat sur les origines des Indo-Européens', in *Eléments*, Spring 1991, pp. 56–59; and Harald Haarmann, 'Contact Linguistics, Archaeology and Ethnogenetics: An Interdisciplinary Approach of the Indo-European Problem', art. cit., pp. 265–288. Cf. also the information published by the journals *Antiquity*, 1988, pp. 454–595, and *Current Anthropology*, June 1988, pp. 437–468 (texts by David W Anthony & Bernard Wailes, Graeme Barker, Robert Coleman, Marija Gimbutas, Andrew Sheratt), as well as the critiques presented by IM Diakonov (*Annual of Armenian Linguistics*, 1988, pp. 79–87), JH Hasanoff (*Language*, 1988, pp. 800–803), KR Norman (*Lingua*, 1988, pp. 91–114), Enrico Campanile (*Kratylos*, 1988, pp. 53–56), Oswald Szemerényi (*Transactions of the Philological Society*, 1989, pp. 156–171), Bernard Sergent (*Annales ESC*, 1990, pp. 388–394), Alexander Häusler (*Zeitschrift für Archäologie*, 1990, pp. 125–128), Edgar C Polomé & John C Kerns (*Mother Tongue*, 1990), etc.

228 *European Economic Prehistory: A New Approach* (New York: Harcourt Brace Jovanovich & London: Academic Press, 1983).

229 *Prehistoric Farming in Europe* (Cambridge: Cambridge University Press, 1985).

For Renfrew, the IE had never supplanted the ancient cultures of 'Old Europe', but were identical to them. The builders of megaliths were also IE. The existence of a pre-IE culture, clearly differentiated from the IE culture of the fourth and third millennia, thus becomes incomprehensible, as does the presence of pre-IE languages surviving here or there, in peripheral or mountainous regions, whether Basque, Iberian, Pictish, or certain Caucasian languages. As for the transition from the cultures of 'Old Europe' to those that result, in the traditional perspective, from their Indo-Europeanisation, this ensues from an internal evolution whose causes remain mysterious. From this point of view, the thesis of Renfrew, which in reality says 'the Indo-Europeans never existed',[230] or which leads to the 'dissolution of the very notion of Indo-European',[231] could also be better qualified as 'Pan-Indo-European': the Indo-Europeans are at once everywhere and nowhere.

Regarding the diffusionist pattern that Renfrew asserts, which radically contradicts his previously published works,[232] the proposed chronol-

---

230 Pierre Enckell, 'Do you speak indo-européen?', in *L'Evénement du jeudi*, 4 October 1990, p. 125.

231 Daniel Dubuisson, 'Ces paysans indo-européens', in *Libération*, 2 October 1990.

232 Recall that a diffusionist pattern is one that postulates a slow diffusion of a new cultural complex, without movements of corresponding people. On the linguistic plane, every diffusionist schematic is bound to reject the Schleicherian model of a derivation by arborescence, adhering to the 'undulatory' model proposed by Johannes Schmidt. In his last book, Colin Renfrew adopts a position rigorously inverse to that which he defended some years earlier in *Before Civilization* (op. cit.). Basing himself on the new C-14 datings, he proposes here, as we have seen, to refute the diffusionist approach once popularised by V Gordon Childe, an approach according to which '[Europe's] development was ascribed instead to a process of the diffusion of culture — that is to say to influences from more civilized lands in the Near East' (p. 31), that is by contacts between neighbouring zones involving the transfer of new ideas and discoveries. It necessarily challenges the idea of any influence exercised over Greece or Europe from the southeast, from Asia Minor: 'We cannot doubt that there had been contact between Greece and, at the same time, the Levant and Egypt from around 3000, but a critical examination raises doubts that there were of any great consequence for society. I believe in fact that this first European civilisation represents a European evolution and that most of its traits can be linked, not to the previous civilisations of the Near East, but to the local antecedents and to the processes at work in the Aegean for the past millennium' [I was unable to find this and the next two citations in the English text; Benoist's refer-

ogy appears untenable. If the Indo-Europeans existed in the seventh millennium, which cannot be ruled out, it is impossible that they could have spread gradually across Europe in this period from an original homeland in Asia Minor. Such a hypothesis, which amounts to an inversion of the commonly accepted meaning of Indo-Europeanisation (from the north or the east towards the south and southwest) contradicts everything that we know about Neolithic European cultures. For example, Renfrew postulates the presence of the IE in Greece from the sixth millennium, while we know perfectly well that they only arrived at the beginning of the third, and there is not the slightest trace of archaeological evidence for an IE migration to the Aegean before the beginning of the second.

If the first IE were the bearers of agriculture, the subordinate role attributed to the productive function in the trifunctional system discovered by Dumézil becomes incomprehensible at one stroke, as does the equally subordinate role occupied in the religious domain by agricultural and chthonic divinities. More generally, the tripartite ideology of the IE, along with what it reveals about the structure of the pantheon, the social stratification of IE societies (human groups who do not know any social hierarchy rarely have hierarchised pantheons), and of 'heroic' values which were honoured, at least in the last common stage, is completely incompatible with the idea of an IE society composed of peaceful farmers. The patriarchal and warlike character of these first IE societies, founded on a system of chiefdoms, is the opposite of what we know of the first agricultural cultures of the Near East. The close similarities that we meet in domains as distant from each other as Vedic India and Celtic Ireland, for example those concerning the rituals for the enthronement of sover-

---

ences to the French edition (*L'énigme indo-européenne: Archéologie et langage* [Paris: Flammarion, 1990]) are used instead — Ed.]. And further: 'It is inaccurate to consider the Minoan-Mycenaean civilisation as "secondary", as derived from the Near East or inspired by it. It was an ancient and original creation in Greece, as much as the Sumerian civilization in Mesopotamia or the Olmec civilization of Mexico' (p. 211). His general conclusion is that 'the development of Europe must be considered in European terms, at least until the second millennium and the beginning of the Bronze Age' (p. 194).

eigns, are also incompatible with the thesis of Renfrew. Such similarities can only be explained by a common heritage, whose source cannot be found in Mesopotamia.

Moreover, if the chief distinctive trait of PIE was the practice of agriculture, we should logically be able to retrieve a great number of agricultural terms in common IE, as well as a large number of terms of IE origin in the vocabulary of the non-IE languages of Asia Minor. This common vocabulary should also contain numerous terms relating to plants cultivated in Mediterranean countries. Finally, if the PIE from Anatolia had made the techniques of agriculture known in the Aegean and in Greece, we would expect from this that agricultural terminology in the Greek language would be predominantly of IE origin. But the opposite is true. While common terms dealing with breeding are numerous, which confirms the pastoral character of PIE culture, the common IE vocabulary is deficient in the agricultural domain: we have the greatest difficulty determining the species which the IE cultivated, and there is not a single name of a fruit tree attested in PIE. It is not even certain that the names for wheat and barley in the IE languages come from a pre-IE substrate or not.[233] The plants, trees, and animals that the IE have met in the Mediterranean have most often been designated by words drawn from the local, pre-IE vocabulary. As to the agricultural vocabulary of the Greek language, it is in essence non-IE (and completely different from the vocabulary of Western IE languages concerning cultivated plants). Lastly, if the PIE had come from Asia Minor, there would by necessity be a common IE name for the 'sea', given that the Mediterranean bathes southern Anatolia. The Proto-Greeks, having known the Mediterranean before having even crossed the Aegean, would not have needed to borrow a non-IE word (*thalassa*) to designate it.

The presence in PIE of common words for realities perfectly unknown in Mesopotamia during the seventh millennium, such as birch or beaver,

---

233 Cf. Edgar C Polomé, 'Indo-European and Substrate Languages in the West', in *Archivio glottologico italiano*, 1992, pp. 71–76.

is equally incompatible with Renfrew's thesis. The central role occupied by the horse in the common IE vocabulary also becomes inexplicable when we know that there were no horses in Anatolia before the fourth millennium, and that the first remains of horses discovered in Greece only date to the beginning of the Bronze Age. The ideogram for 'horse' appears at the beginning of the third millennium in Elamite hieroglyphics, and in the middle of this same millennium in Sumerian cuneiform, but at this date the horse is still unknown in the north of Mesopotamia, where the donkey itself did not appear before 2000. If the IE came from Asia Minor in the seventh millennium, they could not have possessed a common word to designate the horse. As Jean Haudry writes, 'If we assume that Indo-European had been diffused from the seventh millennium by Anatolian farmers, it becomes impossible to explain how realities that were unknown to them are expressed by the same vocable in different Indo-European languages, especially when it is a matter of geographically separated languages, which have not been able to borrow from the same language, and of an unmotivated vocable, which could not have been derived secondarily or in parallel'.[234]

In addition, if Renfrew's thesis were correct, the PIE language would necessarily be attested in one form or another in the first documents written in Mesopotamia, such as the Elamite and Sumerian documents, as well as the oldest written attestations of Semitic languages, like Akkadian in the third millennium or Ugaritic in the second. This is obviously not the case, since no IE presence whatsoever is attested in the region before the beginning of the second millennium. Renfrew's thesis also implies a similarity between PIE and the non-IE languages of Anatolia that is much higher than can actually be observed. It is indeed strange that the first IE speakers, if they had already been present in the region for many thousands of years, had not formed the linguistic substratum that developed itself in the third millennium in the same location (Hatti, Hurrian-Urartian, North Semitic). It is also completely strange that a non-IE substratum can

---

234 'A propos d'un livre récent', in *Etudes indo-européennes*, 10, 1991, p. 214.

be observed in the IE languages of Anatolia, whether Hittite or Luwian, while they are supposed to have developed without any interruption from the seventh millennium at the site of their original homeland. The fact that no ancient language of the Near East outside Anatolia is IE already constitutes an insurmountable obstacle for Renfrew's thesis, for we cannot see how the influence of PIE would not also be applied towards the south. Finally, if the IE had been overwhelmingly present from the seventh millennium in Asia Minor, and then the Aegean and the Greek Peninsula, we fail to comprehend how the non-IE languages could still have been present, sometimes even in a dominant position, around 1900 BCE in Anatolia and around 1500 BCE in Greece.

Lying immediately adjacent to the original homeland assumed by Renfrew, the Armenian language should logically present some particularly archaic IE features. However, this is not the case, even though the Armenians have practically never budged from their territory. We have seen from the fact of their archaism that the Armenian languages were deprived of a certain number of characteristic traits of common IE. Now these traits are present in Armenian and Phrygian; however, for Renfrew they are supposed to be immediate derivations. As James P Mallory humorously wrote, if the Renfrew's thesis were to coincide with what we know of the Armenian language, we would have to imagine that it took 5000 years for the Proto-Indo-Europeans to cross the one or two hundred kilometres that separate them from Armenia.[235] No one can actually imagine that Armenian already existed in the seventh or sixth millennium, or that it had been spoken from this date without any interruption. The same is true for the Greek language, which is the closest language to Armenian. Renfrew also takes up the idea that the Indo-Europeans had already penetrated into western Pakistan and into the Indus Valley at the end of the seventh millennium. But in this case, it is the kinship of Vedic Sanskrit with Greek and Indo-Iranian, and the fact that the three languages also contain a great number of isoglosses, which becomes inexplicable. If the Hittites and Mycenaean Greeks represent the immediate continuation of

---

235 *In Search of the Indo-Europeans,* op. cit., p. 178.

the first farmers of Anatolia, how could we account, on one hand, for the fundamental differences which appear between Greek and Anatolian at every level of the language, and on the other hand, for the remarkable correspondences that exist to the contrary between Greek and Indo-Iranian? We will note finally that Renfrew deliberately eliminates all references to the Baltic group, whose archaism and linguistic conservatism alone contradict his hypothesis, and that in his approach, the extremely ancient connections between PIE and the Finno-Ugric language families, and the fact that PIE would be closer to Uralian than any other linguistic family, also becomes inexplicable.

The final inconvenience for Renfrew's thesis is that there is not the least archaeological trace of the homeland that he proposes. Renfrew contents himself to evoke on this subject a population that would have lived 'before about 6000 years BC [...] in the eastern part of Anatolia, and in some adjacent lands to the east and south-east'.[236] This is vague. We can conclude that, in the best case, Renfrew has only retraced the history of the diffusion of agriculture in Europe, but not its Indo-Europeanisation. 'The thesis according to which the original Indo-European homeland is situated in a zone containing southeastern Europe, Anatolia, Transcaucasia, and North Mesopotamia', writes Marija Gimbutas, 'cannot be accepted for a simple reason: the greatest Neolithic civilisations of this region represent the antithesis of every characteristic that it is possible to attribute to the Proto-Indo-Europeans on the basis of mythological research and comparative linguistics'.[237] 'Anatolia', concludes James P Mallory, 'is the wrong place at the wrong time and migrations from it give the wrong results'.[238]

On the geographic plane, the thesis of Thomas V Gamkrelidze and Vjaceslas V Ivanov[239] do not differ fundamentally from that of Renfrew:

---

236 *Archaeology and Language*, op. cit., p. 266.

237 'Primary and Secondary Homeland of the Indo-Europeans', in *JIES*, Spring–Summer 1985, p. 185.

238 *In Search of the Indo-Europeans*, op. cit., p. 181.

239 Werner Winter & Richard A Rhodes (eds.), *Indo-European and the Indo-Europeans: A Reconstruction and Historical Analysis of a Proto-Language and a Proto-Culture*, 2 vols. (Berlin-New York: Mouton de Gruyter, 1995); 'The Ancient Near East and the Indo-European Question: Temporal and Territorial Characteristics of Proto-

the homeland is situated, according to them, between the southern Causasus, eastern Anatolia, and northern Mesopotamia. But the chronology that they adopt is completely different, since they place the final common habitat in the fifth or fourth millennium. In this context, the Indo-Europeans are first established on the steppes of the Volga and the North-Pontic region, before dispersing towards Central and Western Europe. The Proto-Greeks would be directed first towards the Balkans, before descending again into the Greek Peninsula. Unlike Renfrew, who is an archaeologist, Gamkrelidze and Ivanov did not reject the achievements of linguistic palaeontology. On the contrary, they based themselves essentially on linguistic data, making appeal to the glottalic theory and to a system of phonology reconstructed in a completely different way to the classical approach. They also attribute a grand importance to the interactions that would occur between the IE languages, the Kartvelian languages (Caucasian), and the Semitic languages.

This model has gained no significant conviction due to its largely speculative character. The phonological system upon which Gamkrelidze and Ivanov based it has been strongly criticised by DM Diakonov.[240] Other authors have remarked that the 'interactions' supposedly supporting a single stem of Proto-Semitic, Proto-Kartvelian, and PIE, assuming they even took place, could only have occurred much earlier, that is, before the formation of the PIE community. Gamkrelidze and Ivanov have on the other hand been forced to recognise that, in the region that they believe they can identify as the homeland, there exists 'no archaeological culture which can be identified in an explicit fashion with the Proto-Indo-Europeans.'[241] For lack of anything better, they have proposed to identify this homeland with the agricultural culture of Halaf, which developed

Indo-European Based on Linguistics and Historico-Cultural Data', in *JIES*, Spring–Summer 1985; and Thomas V Gamkrelidze, 'Proto-Indo-Europeans in Anatolia', in *JIES*, Autumn–Winter 1989, pp. 341–350.

240 'On the Original Home of the Speakers of Indo-European', in *Soviet Anthropology and Archaeology*, Autumn 1984, pp. 5–87 (reprinted in *JIES*, Spring–Summer 1985, pp. 92–174).

241 'The Ancient Near East and the Indo-European Question', art. cit., p. 31.

in Upper Mesopotamia from the fifth millennium. This position cannot be accepted by any serious archaeologist. As Marija Gimbutas recalled, the Neolithic civilisations that existed in Transcaucasia or in northern Mesopotamia, the upper basin of the Euphrates, are the exact antithesis of those that linguistic palaeontology and the comparative history of religions teach us about the first IE societies.

Today, IM Diakonov[242] is almost the only one defending the thesis of an original Balkan habitat. According to him, PIE would be diffused by gradual 'waves of advancement' from a Balkano-Danubian agricultural civilisation from the fifth and fourth millennia. This hypothesis does not fare better than that of Renfrew, and for much the same reasons.[243] Any theory situating the homeland in the Balkans implies the existence of enduring contacts between the PIE (at least on the southern and eastern margins) and the Pre-IE languages of Aegean origin, contacts that would have necessarily left traces. If we do in fact find traces of these Aegean languages in Greek, we find none in common IE.

The Kurgan Culture

The thesis sustained from 1966 by the archaeologist of Lithuanian origin, Marija Gimbutas (1921–1994), is more serious. Gimbutas places the original homeland in the large area of steppes and forests that stretch from southern Russia and Ukraine to the north of the Caspian and Black seas. She identifies the PIE people with the Kurgan culture, who interred their dead in chambers of earth or stone covered with a tumulus (mound). This culture, whose IE character is undisputed by anyone, finds its origin in the region of the Urals and the lower course of the Volga, and more distantly in the steppes of central Russian Asia and of western Turkmenistan. From the middle of the fifth millennium, the Kurgan people, via a series of migratory waves, progressively spread their funerary rites throughout Europe, along with the metallurgy of bronze, a pantheon dominated by

---

242 'On the Original Home of the Speakers of Indo-European', art. cit.

243 Cf. James P Mallory, *In Search of the Indo-Europeans*, op. cit., p. 181.

celestial gods, a symbolic system having the Sun as a central motif, a patriarchal and patrilocal model of society, a pastoral way of life, and the use
of the domestic horse and chariot.

This thesis, which places the homeland on the steppes of southern
Russia between the beginning of the Neolithic and the Bronze Age,
had already been affirmed by Otto Schrader in 1883. It was taken up by
a number of researchers after him. On the eve of the First World War,
Gorodtsof articulated its modern formulation by proposing to define the
'Pre-Scythian' cultural development of southern Russia according to the
succession of pit-graves (*jamno*) and wooden burial chambers (*srubno*).
In 1961, Nikolaj J Merpert followed by proposing a chronology of the
Neolithic in Russia based not only on stratigraphy, but on typological
comparison. Instead of the traditional expression 'culture of ochre tombs'
(German *Ockergrabkultur*), we now begin to speak of a 'pit-grave culture'
(French *culture des tombes à fosse*, Russian *jamnaja kultura*) divided into
four periods. In 1956, Gimbutas gave the name 'Kurgan culture' to this
cultural complex, which, between 4500 and 2900, saw the formation, development, and expansion of the PIE community.

The burial mounds (Russian *kurgan*, 'mound, tumulus') are tombs
consisting of a pit topped with the dugout earth, first lined and covered
by a cairn (a pile of stones), then by a circular tumulus. These tombs often
contain red ochre, as well as funerary furnishings attesting to a highly
differentiated society: spearheads and arrows, knives and daggers of flint,
emblems of power, horse-headed sceptres, torques, jewellery, pottery,
and so on.[244] They harboured quite large skeletons, either supine or half-
seated. Inhumation in the flexed position, to the right for men, to the left
for women, only appears in the first half of the fourth millennium, a clean
break with the previous mode of inhumation (where the dead were buried in the foetal position). We note a strong predominance of individual

---

244 Cf. James P Mallory, 'Social Structure in the Pontic-Caspian Eneolithic: A
Preliminary Review', in *JIES*, Spring–Summer 1990, pp. 15–57; and Karlene Jones-
Bley, 'So That Fame Might Live Forever — The Indo-European Burial Tradition',
ibid., pp. 215–224.

tombs over collective tombs, a phenomenon which is also radically new in comparison to the previous funerary practices. It is the distribution of these characteristic graves, which we originally find in the steppes of the Volga-Caspian region, that allowed Marija Gimbutas to correlate the expansion of the IE with the appearance of tumulus tombs among the Mycenaean Greeks, the Phrygians, the Macedonians, the Thracians, and the Venetics.

It seems that in Ukraine during the period of 5000/3500 BCE, the Dnieper formed a distinct ethnolinguistic frontier between two different types of cultures. On one side, west of the river, was the Cucuteni-Tripolye culture (Moldavia and western Ukraine), which included some relatively significant agglomerations (at least a thousand houses spread over 350 or 400 hectares). Its inhabitants practiced agriculture, honoured principally feminine divinities, and produced highly refined pottery. On the other side, east of the Dnieper, were more sparse populations which raised live-stock and led an above all pastoral way of life. They honoured celestial divinities, interred their dead in tumulus graves, ate and sacrificed horses, and produced more rudimentary pottery. The Cucuteni-Tripolye culture, which derived from the other cultures of the Copper Age situated more to the southwest, in the Carpathians and the Balkans, had been one of the principal cultures that Marija Gimbutas referred to as 'Old Europe', whereas the cultures situated west of the Dnieper, which archaeologists called the cultures of Dnieper-Donetz II (5000/4500 BCE) and of Sredny Stog (4500/3500 BCE), would have constituted the cradle of the PIE.[245] In fact, just as she speaks of the 'Kurgan tradition', subsuming in a unitary complex most of the Pontic cultures usually distinguished by archaeolo-gists, Gimbutas, under the expression 'Old Europe', designates an entire series of Chalcolithic cultures from southeastern Europe, the basin of the

---

245 Cf. Mircea Radulescu, 'La culture Cucuteni et les Indo-Européens', in *La civilisation de Cucuteni en contexte européen* (Iassy: Alexandru Ioan Cuza University, 1987), pp. 237–252.

Danube, the Balkans, and the Aegean Sea.[246] 'Old Europe', whose apogee
seems to be somewhere between 5000 and 4000 BCE (the emergence of
long-distance trade, the opening of copper and gold mines, refinement of
clothing and lifestyle, polychromatic ceramics, etc.), corresponds to the
complex of Danubian culture which finds its origin in the Neolithisation
of the Balkans in the seventh millennium, whose most accomplished
form, two thousand years later, was the Starčevo-Körös culture (Hungary,
Romania, Balkans). Besides the Cucuteni-Tripolye culture, it also included the Karanovo culture from Maritsa Valley in Bulgaria, whose
influence reached to the Danubian plains and the Aegean Sea; the Vinča
culture, which succeeded the Neolithic Starčevo culture in the Balkans;
the Lengyel culture in the basin of the middle Danube; that of the Butmir
in Bosnia; Petreşti in Transylvania; and Tiszapolgár in Hungary and western Romania, and so on.

Contrary to the identification of the cultures of 'Old Europe' with the
first IE farmers, as Renfrew supposed, the arrival of the IE would have
drawn the flourishing of these first, great European agricultural civilisations to a brutal close. Gimbutas, who has never hidden her sympathy
for the cultures of 'Old Europe', particularly due to their 'gynaecocratic'
character, has repeatedly underscored their antithetical character in relation to PIE culture. These cultures are characterised by a sedentary and
predominantly urban habitat, a high artistic level, and a relatively peaceful way of life. They honour essentially feminine and chthonic divinities
(goddesses of fertility and fecundity, the Great Mother, bird and serpent
goddesses), and present matrilineal, matrifocal, and matrilocal structures,

---

246 Marija Gimbutas, 'The Kurgan Culture', in *Actes du VIIe Congrès international des
sciences préhistoriques et protohistoriques, Prague, 21-27 août 1966*, Prague 1970, vol.
1, pp. 483-487; 'Old Europe c. 7000-3500 B.C.: The Earliest Civilization Before the
Infiltration of Indo-European Peoples', in *JIES*, 1973, 1; *Goddesses and Gods of Old
Europe, 6500-3500 B.C.* (Berkeley-Los Angeles: University of California Press, 1982);
and 'The Social Structure of Old Europe', in *JIES*, Autumn-Winter 1989, pp. 197-214.
Due to the importance of the urban habitat in the cultures of 'Old Europe', Sorin
Paliga ('Proto-Indo-European, Pre-Indo-European, Old European: Archaeological
Evidence and Linguistic Investigation', in *JIES*, Autumn-Winter 1989, pp. 309-334)
has proposed to denominate them 'Urian' or 'Urban'.

whose survivals we can observe into the historical period.[247] As egalitarian, theocentric, and matricentric societies, they contrast sharply with the
first IE cultures, which are characterised by an above all pastoral economy,
combining agriculture and the raising of livestock, a sparse habitat, small
villages and fortresses, large rectangular houses, mostly undecorated pottery, horse sacrifice and the cult of fire, a pantheon dominated by celestial divinities and gods of thunder, an endogamy enhanced by marriages
among crossed cousins with a network of allegiances and reciprocal de-
pendencies, families gathered into clans and tribes, a system of chiefdoms,
a social hierarchy placing a caste of priest-magicians at the summit and
a group of farmers and cattle or horse-breeders at the base, and so on.
'The cultures of Old Europe and of the Kurgan', writes Gimbutas, 'are opposed to each other. Old Europe characterises itself by large clusters and
an economy of sedentary horticulture; the Kurgan culture, by mobility
and small villages. The first is matrilineal, egalitarian, and peaceful; the
second, patriarchal, hierarchised, and warlike. Each of the two ideologies has created a different set of gods and symbols. The ideology of old
Europe places the accent on the eternal aspects of birth, death, and re-
generation symbolised by a feminine principle: the creative Mother. The
patriarchal ideology of the Kurgans (known from the comparative study
of Indo-European mythology), is founded on the virile and warlike gods
of the bright, revolving sky. The Old Europeans were not interested in of-
fensive weapons, whereas the Kurgans, like all Indo-Europeans, glorified
the sword'.[248]

---

247 We notably find traces in Crete and in the islands of the Aegean (Lesbos, Lemnos,
     Naxos, Kos), where the rule of matrilineal succession has remained in effect since
     the end of the eighteenth century, whereas among the non-IE populations of Europe
     like the Picts (inhabitants of Great Britain before the Celts) and the Basque, but also
     among the Celtic (cult of the *Matres*), the Germanic, and the Baltic peoples. Cf.
     Michael Everson, 'Tenacity in Religion, Myth and Folklore: The Neolithic Goddess
     of Old Europe Preserved in a Non-Indo-European Setting', in *JIES*, Autumn–Winter
     1989, pp. 277–295.
248 'La fin de l'Europe ancienne', in *La Recherche*, March 1978, p. 230.

Gimbutas explains the rise of the Kurgan culture by the use of the domestic warhorse and chariot, or two-wheeled cart, as well as the general superiority of weaponry and an extraordinary mobility. 'The process of Indo-Europeanisation", she emphasises, "was not physical, but cultural. It must be understood as a military victory that consisted in the successful imposition of a new religion, a new language, and a new administrative system upon the autochthonous groups'.[249]

At a conference on the IE organised in 1966 in Philadelphia, Marija Gimbutas proposed a detailed chronology of the Kurgan culture and the principal migrations to which it gave birth.[250] The beginning of the first phase (Kurgan I), which extends to around 4400/4300 BCE, remains uncertain. After deriving it from the culture of the Kuban in the Caucasus during the 1950s, Gimbutas then placed the origin of the Kurgan culture in the steppes of Kazakhstan and by the course of the lower Volga, going so far as to assimilate it to the Afanasjevo culture in central Siberia. The stone tools of Kurgan I recall those from sites east of the Caspian, and their users could be the ancient Mesolithic populations of Dzhebel established upon the Volga. During this period, the Kurgan culture reached towards Ukraine, where it would have covered the Neolithic culture of Dnieper-Donetz in its second stage. It is characterised by covered graves, not yet Kurgan properly speaking, but with a cairn.

Kurgan II would cover the period 4300/4000 BCE and would have seen a first extension towards the Danube. The Kurgan funerary rites now begin to be generalised, at the same time as new symbols of a solar inspiration emerge everywhere (notably the double spiral, which we rediscover on numerous anthropomorphic steles, as far as the Swiss Alps, including Val Camonica). The settlements are transformed, the pastoral

---

249 'Primary and Secondary Homeland of the Indo-Europeans', art. cit., p. 196.

250 'Proto-Indo-European Culture: The Kurgan Culture during the Fifth, Fourth and Third Millenia B.C.', in George Cardona, Henry M Hoenigswald, & Alfred Senn (eds.), *Indo-European and Indo-Europeans*, op. cit., pp. 155–197; 'The Indo-Europeans: Archaeological Problems', in *American Anthropologist*, 1963, pp. 815–836; and 'An Archaeologist's View of PIE in 1975', art. cit., pp. 289–307.

character of the economy is accentuated, new metallurgical techniques make their appearance, while the Proto-Europoid skeleton type asserts itself more distinctly. It is during this epoch that we see the disappearance of the Polgar culture in the northeast of Hungary and Transylvania, and the Cortaillod-Lagozza culture in Switzerland and north Italy. Because Sredny Stog was one of the principal sites of the Dnieper-Donetz culture, Russian archaeologists brought Kurgan I and Kurgan II under the name Sredny Stog II culture, which they situate in the lower course of the Dnieper and the Don.

For Russian archaeologists, Kurgan III (4000/3200) corresponds to the Usatovo-Mikhajlovka I culture, to the north of the Black Sea, and to the beginning of the Majkop, which is the early stage of the pit-tomb culture (*drevnejamna kultura*). The graveyards of this period hold between four and twenty-five tumulus tombs, in which the bodies are entombed in a flexed position. The exploitation of copper intensifies. The chariot takes on such importance that it is occasionally buried with the dead: the wheels are placed in the four corners of the funerary pit, while the yoke and harness are arranged over the tomb, all being covered by the tumulus. The destruction of the cultures of Old Europe culminate in the last stage, Kurgan IV (3200/2900 BCE), which Russian archaeologists identify with the culture of pit-graves properly speaking (*jamnaya kultura*), or the Yamna cultural complex, between the lower Dnieper and the lower Volga.

Gimbutas then distinguishes three great waves of migration,[251] whose successions trace a vast scenario of progressive 'Kurganisation' of the largest portion of Europe. The first imposes itself around 4400/4200 BCE, which is the hinge of Kurgan I and Kurgan II. It first hits the north of the Azov Sea and the Dnieper region, where the Kurgan people inflict themselves on the local population of hunters and fishermen, giving birth to the culture of Sredny Stog. They next reach the valley of the lower Danube, Bulgaria, Romania, eastern Hungary, the plain of Maritsa, and

---

251 'The Three Waves of the Kurgan People into Old Europe', in *Archives suisses d'anthropologie générale*, 1979, pp. 113–117.

Macedonia. The culture of Karanovo VI, south of Moldavia and in the course of the lower Danube, is completely disrupted, and its members are forced to flee West from Romania over the lands of the Vinča culture. The result of this is a whole series of upheavals in Yugoslavia, Hungary, and Czechoslovakia: the Vinča population is repelled to the west of Hungary (the Balaton group), as well as Croatia, Bosnia, and Slavonia (the Lasinja group), while the representatives of the Tiszapolgár culture spilled into Transylvania, and those of the Lengyel culture emigrated towards the upper Danube, Poland, and Germany. The Karanovo culture will be replaced in the lower Danube, east of Romania and in Bulgaria, by a complex cultural mixture, Cernavodă I, combining the Kurgan elements from the steppes with a substratum from the Karanovo (Gumelniţa) cultures. This is how the first 'Kurganised' cultures appear in Central Europe from the end of the Neolithic. The Cucuteni-Tripolye culture is, by contrast, spared: archaeology reveals a coexistence between the Kurgan and the Cucuteni people for a thousand years.

The second wave took place around 3400/3200 BCE, at the end of Kurgan III,[252] expanding itself in all directions from the territory already 'Kurganised' northwest of the Black Sea, where it formed the Usatovo culture, an amalgamation of the Kurgan culture and the Cucuteni culture. This second phase strikes towards the south, towards the Cernavoda I culture, whose representatives are forced to recede towards the south and east, establishing themselves in Macedonia, Bulgaria, and as far as western Anatolia, notably on the site of Troy. The Cucuteni-Tripolye culture is overwhelmed this time. In the Balkans, the Vinča, Butmir, and Petresti cultures are displaced. A new cultural entity develops itself in the basin of the Danube and the Balkans from Cernavodă I and its fusion with the ancient cultures of 'Old Europe'. We give them the name Cernavodă III in Romania, Boleráz in western Slovakia, and Baden in the basin of the middle Danube. Realising a vast 'Balko-Danubian' cultural complex, its

---

252 Cf. Marija Gimbutas, 'The Kurgan Wave #2 (c. 3400–3200 B.C.) into Europe and the Following Transformation of Culture', in *JIES*, Autumn–Winter 1980, pp. 273–315.

influence extends through the entire basin of the Danube, from Romania and Bulgaria, to Yugoslavia, Hungary, Czechoslovakia, Austria, southern Germany, and central Germany as high as Lake Constance and the Nördlinger Ries, where it will give birth to Furchenstich earthenware and the type called Rössen III. In the middle of the fourth millennium, the 'Kurganisation' of the upper basin of the Danube resulted in the emergence of the Mondsee, Altheim, and Pfyn cultures. The Kurgan funeral rites imposed themselves in the region of the Elbe and the Saale, as well as Bohemia. Parallel to this, elements of the Kurgan culture spread into the northern plain, sparking a transformation of the Funnel Beaker culture that will in turn give birth to Globular Amphorae, and then to Corded Ware. In the last quarter of the fourth millennium, the entire cultural map of Europe is disrupted. The culture of 'Old Europe' only subsists in the Danube region in the form of a few rare islands, such as the complex of Coțofeni.

The third wave, around 3000/2800 BCE, is more powerful still. It resulted in the destruction of the Baden culture in Central Europe, and in the multiplication of pit-graves in Romania, Yugoslavia, and eastern Hungary. At the beginning of the third millennium, the culture of 'Old Europe' is progressively eliminated from the Greek Peninsula and the Aegean, and only succeeded in maintaining itself in Crete and the Cyclades. 'From the moment that the Indo-Europeans occupied Greece', Gimbutas states, 'the culture of Old Europe only remained intact in the Cyclades and in Crete. There it continued to flourish until the middle of the second millennium BCE, where it was destroyed by the eruption of the local volcano at Thera, and elsewhere, by the Mycenaeans, who invaded the Cyclades, conquering Knossos and appropriating it for themselves.[253] Finally, the expansion of the Kurgan people gave birth, on its eastern fringes, to the Poltavka culture along the Samara, and to the Sintashta and Petrovka cultures. These latter would have formed the basis of the Andronovo culture, which

---

253 'La fin de l'Europe ancienne', art. cit., p. 235.

would extend to the borders of Iran and Afghanistan, which we consider to be the 'ancestral' culture of the Indo-Iranian group.

In this scheme, Indo-Europeanisation thus follows the progress of 'Kurganisation'. The first wave of migration resulted in the Anatolian group. The second gave birth to the Phrygians, the Germans, the Balto-Slavs, the Illyrians, and the Celts. The third produced the Daco-Thracians, the Greeks, the Armenians, and the Indo-Iranians. The Germanic, Baltic, Slavic, Celtic, Italic, Illyrian, and Phrygian tribes all derive from the Kurgan culture by the intermediary of the Corded Ware culture. The Indo-Iranians are linked via the intermediary of the Andronovo culture. The Celtic civilisation, who appear with the Urnfield culture, extended by the Hallstatt culture and La Tène, would result from the intermediary of the Unetice culture, and from there, the Vučedol culture, who found their origin in the Baden culture, born from the 'Kurganisation' of local elements of 'Old Europe'.

In this scenario, Gimbutas insists strongly on the role of the horse and chariot: the domestication of the horse was the essential cause and principal vector of the Kurgan people's expansion from the wooded steppes of the North Caspian and the Black Sea. For Gimbutas, this domestication would occur during the sixth millennium in an area stretching from the valley of the Don to the plains of northern Kazakhstan. The domestic horse was further distributed in Europe by the Kurgan people in the second half of the fourth millennium, then in Central Asia in the third millennium, and finally in India and Anatolia in the second millennium. This assertion has given rise to numerous debates. The bones of horses have indeed been retrieved from Kurgan tombs in the region of the lower Dnieper, dating from 4400 BCE, as well as in sites dating to around 5500 BCE belonging to the Samara culture. These are the most ancient remains which we have attesting to the direct relation between man and horse, but we do not have proof that they are the remains of domestic horses. The remains of a horse whose premolars bear some traces of a bit have, however, been recently discovered between the Dnieper and the Don, at the level of the village Dereivka, on a site belonging to the Sredny Stog culture, which we have been able to date to the period of 4200/3800 BCE. These remains, studied from 1989 by Anthony W Smith and DR Brown, presently belong to the oldest domestic horse that we know in the world.[254] For Anthony W Smith, the centre of horse domestication is best sought in the steppes of the northern Black Sea region. It is possible that the horse had first been used as a beast of burden, before being used as a mount or for drawing chariots.

It is certain that the horse occupied a central place among the PIE, both in everyday life as well as in the politico-religious domain, as testified by a number of rituals (the *ashvamedha* in Vedic India, the Roman rite of the *Equus October*, the sacrifice of the horse on the occasion of the enthroning of the kings of Ulster, etc.), as well by the name of the Celtic goddess Epona, the name Hengist and Horsa in the Euhemeristic account of the Saxon conquest of England, and a certain number of personal names (Indian Ashvacakra, Old Persian and Avestan Vishtaspa, Greek Hipparchos and Philippos, Gallic Epopennus, Old English Eomaer), etc.[255] The divine IE twins (the Greek Dioskouri and Molions or Aktorions, the Vedic Ashvins, and the Germanic Alces, retransposed to Rome under the 'mythohistoric' figures of Romulus and Remus) are themselves frequently presented as hippomorphs or as 'possessors of horses' (an epithet

---

254 Cf. David W Anthony, 'Horse, Wagon, and Chariot: Indo-European Languages and Archaeology', in *Antiquity*, September 1995; and 'Digging Up Language: The Archaeology of Indo-European Origins', unpublished article, 1996, pp. 14–16. MA Levine ('Dereivka and the Problem of Horse Domestication', in *Antiquity*, 1990, pp. 727–740) asserts that they are in fact the remains of a wild horse, of a type known since the Upper Palaeolithic. David W Anthony & DR Brown ('The Origins of Horseback Riding', in *Antiquity*, 1991, pp. 22–38) maintains the opposite. Alexander Häusler feels for his part that the horse remains discovered in the tombs of the Kurgan culture are not numerous enough to justify the importance that Gimbutas attributes to the horse in the expansion of the IE. Cf. also Sándor Bökönyi, 'The Earliest Waves of Domestic Horses in East Europe', in *JIES*, 1978, pp. 17–76; Dimitri Yakolevich Telegin & David W Anthony, 'The "Kurgan" Culture: Indo-European Origins, and the Domestication of the Horse; A Reconsideration', in *Current Anthropology*, 1986, pp. 291–313.

255 Cf. Johannes Meringer, 'The Horse in the Art and Ideology of the Indo-European Peoples', in *JIES*, 1981, pp. 178–204.

of the Ashvins in the Vedas),[256] or even further as the children, brothers, or husbands of hippomorphic goddesses, which allows us to connect the symbolism of the bridle or harness to the couple.[257] Wolfgang Meid has emphasised that such facts prevent us from viewing the horse as a late cultural import among the IE; by necessity, it reflects a common reality.

The military use of the horse is attested among the Hittites towards 2050 BCE. The Aryans of Mitanni, who lived in Mesopotamia in contact with the Hurrians, seem to have made horse-breeding known, and they spread the use of the war chariot throughout the Near East from the fifteenth century BCE. It is also in Hittite that we find the first treatise on horse-breeding. It deals with the text of Kikkuli,[258] who goes back to the fourteenth century. We do not find the IE name of the horse, but the Sumerian word ANSHE.KUR.RA. In Hittite hieroglyphics, however, we find the form *asuua-* (Luwian hieroglyphics *a-su-wa*), which could be related to IE *ekwos-* without requiring a loan from Aryan Mitanni *asva-.*[259]

---

256 In the *Rig Veda*, the Ashvins are twin gods who have the bodies of humans but the heads of horses. They are said to ride across the sky in a golden chariot just before dawn. — Ed.

257 Cf. Cristiano Grottanelli, 'Yoked Horses, Twins, and the Powerful Lady: India, Greece, Ireland and Elsewhere', in *JIES*, Spring–Summer 1986, pp. 125–152. The Germanic Alkes represent particularly archaic divine twins, associated originally with the elk (German *alhi-*), as Hellmut Rosenfeld showed ('Die vandalischen Alkes "Elchreiter", der ostgermanische Hirschkult und die Dioskuren', in *Germanisch-Romanische Monatsschrift*, 1940, pp. 245–258). Cf. also the article 'Dioskuren', in *Reallexikon der Germanischen Altertumskunde*, vol. 5, 1984, pp. 482–484. The harness of the elk of the Germanic Dioscures confirms the relatively late character of the appearance of the domestic horse among the Western IE. Georges Dumézil has shown that the divine twins are linked in the tripartite system to the third function. Regarding the couple formed by each pair of divine twins, we can ask whether there is any room to envisage a binary differentiation, such as we find at the level of the first and second function. Cf. Donald Ward, *The Divine Twins: An Indo-European Myth in Germanic Tradition* (Berkeley-Los Angeles: University of California Press, 1968).

258 Kikkuli was a Hurrian horse trainer who wrote a text on the subject in Hittite which survives. The text dates to 1400 BCE. — Ed.

259 Cf. Annelies Kammenhuber, *Hippologia Hethitica* (Wiesbaden: Otto Harrassowitz, 1961). In his etymological dictionary of Hittite, Jaan Puhvel also mentions a West Semitic form *su:su*, 'horse'.

The PIE name of the 'horse', *ekwos*- (*ëk'uos*) is attested in almost all the other IE languages: Sanskrit *ashva*-, Avestan *aspa*-, Old Persian *asa*-, Tocharian A *yuk*, Tocharian B *yakwe*, Mycenaean *i-qo*, Greek *hippos*, Latin *equus*, Venetic *eku*-, Old English *eoh*, Gaulish *epo*-, Old Irish *ech*, Welsh *ebol*, and so on. Jürgen Untermann[260] believes that the existence of this term does not suffice to demonstrate that the IE had known the horse in its domestic form. Wolfgang Meid[261] and Bernfried Schlerath believe that examination of the lexicon does not allow us to settle this issue. However, the common IE name for horse, derived from a root perhaps evoking 'speed', does not present traits characteristic of an archaic nominal subject, as is the case for the names of the pig, the cow, the bull, and so on. Its thematic vowel is late. In addition, the designations for the horse in different IE languages almost always place it in relation to man (cf. the compound **ekwo-wiro-*, 'men and horses', indicating the chariotry). This varied evidence suggests that the horse known by the PIE was indeed the domestic horse, but that its domestication took place at a relatively late date. Some authors believe to have found confirmation in the fact that most of the IE languages designate the mare with a simple, feminine ending of the word for horse, without giving it a particular name, as is generally the case with the females of wild species. It is also possible that there were different words to designate the domestic horse and the wild horse.

In PIE we find common names for 'chariot', 'wheel', 'harness', 'axle', 'shaft', 'drive a harness' (**wegh-*), and so on. These names are particularly important, for they can help date the last common IE habitat. According to Franz Specht,[262] these terms result from a series of transfers and metaphors from words originally having a different meaning, and he estimates that the last period of PIE unity could be dated on the basis of the common vocabulary concerning wheeled vehicles. These do not appear anywhere

---

260 'Ursprache und historische Realität: Der Beitrag der Indogermanistik zu Fragen der Ethnogenese', in *Studien zur Ethnogenese*, 1985, p. 153.

261 *Archäologie und Sprachwissenschaft*, op. cit.

262 *Der Ursprung der indogermanischen Deklination* (Göttingen: Vandenhoeck & Ruprecht, 1944), pp. 99–103.

in the world before the fifth millennium. The most ancient wagon burial has been discovered on a site from the Kurgan II epoch (4300/4000 BCE). The chariot, then the wagon, would then be spread throughout Central Europe in the following millennium. However, some authors hesitate to place the use of the chariot before 3500 BCE.[263] It is this that leads David W Anthony[264] to believe that the PIE community must still be relatively unified at this date. Against this reasoning, it has been objected that four different IE roots exist to designate the wheel, which could suggest that it is not a matter of one common word, but David W Anthony has reduced their number to two.

A Secondary Homeland?

What Marija Gimbutas' theory has going for it is that it is compatible with our knowledge of the 'distance' that separates the different IE languages. She has the merit of linking the expansion of the IE to population movements for which there are frequently (but not always) attested archaeological traces. She places the cradle of the IE in a territory where the flora and fauna do not contradict what we know of their original environment. Finally, in its broad lines, it is in harmony with the information that we possess regarding the PIE culture. As the IE character of the Kurgan culture is undisputed, numerous researchers have supported the solution that she proposes, not without adding some minor corrections or nuances. This is notably the case with Homer L Thomas, Antonio Tovar, Francisco Rodriguez Adrado, André Martinet, Wolfgang Meid, Vittore Pisani, Winfred P Lehmann, Jak Yakar, Mircea Eliade, Anthony W Smith,

---

263 Stuart Piggott (*The Earliest Wheeled Transport from the Atlantic Coast to the Caspian Sea* [Ithaca, NY: Cornell University Press, 1983]) thinks that the chariot was invented, in the form of a kind of 'wheeled sled', in the Near East at the end of the fourth millennium, and that it only afterwards spread in Europe. The invention of the chariot in the fourth millennium on the Armenian plateau has sometimes been qualified as 'archaeological legend' by IM Diakonov. Cf. also Edgar C Polomé, 'Indo-European and Substrate Languages in the West', in *Archivio glottologico italiano*, 1992, pp. 67–68.

264 'The Archaeology of Indo-European Origins', in *JIES*, 1991, pp. 193–222.

James P Mallory, Bruce Lincoln, A Diebold, and Martin E Huld, among others. Bernard Sergent, who found the hypothesis 'seductive' fifteen years ago,[265] finds it 'decisive' today.[266] David W Anthony,[267] who situates the original homeland in the Lviv-Kiev corridor between 4500 and 3500 BCE, only holds reservations about the chronology and the magnitude of the different waves of invasion. James P Mallory adopts a more or less identical position.

Other authors refuse, however, to adopt the hypothesis of Gimbutas. According to them, the Kurgan culture only constituted a secondary centre of IE expansion, and cannot be identified with the original homeland. This is notably the case with Ward H Goodenough, István Ecsedy, Rüdiger Schmitt, János Makkay, Jean Haudry, Andrew Sherratt, Alexander Häusler, Lothar Kilian, Carl Heinz Böttcher, John C Kernes, Aron Dolgopolsky, and RA Crossland, among others. Ward H Goodenough asserts that 'the Kurgan I people were not *the* Proto-Indo-European people, but a subgroup of these people'.[268] Rüdiger Schmitt,[269] who allies himself with this opinion, suggests that the Kurgan culture is not the only possible candidate for the PIE community. According to James P Mallory's summary of these critiques, '[A]lmost all of the arguments for invasion and cultural transformations are far better explained without reference to Kurgan expansions, and most of the evidence so far presented is either totally con-

---

265 'It is obviously impossible', he adds, 'to affirm that none of the people of the Kurgan culture were Indo-European, or, inversely, that they were—even in the fifth millennium—all Indo-Europeans'. ('Penser—et mal penser—les Indo-Européens', in *Annales ESC*, July–August 1982, pp. 672–673).

266 *Les Indo-Européens*, op. cit., p. 395. Cf. also Jacques Freu, 'L'arrivée des Indo-Européens en Europe', in *Bulletin de l'Association Guillaume Budé*, 1989, pp. 3–41.

267 'The Archaeology of Indo-European Origins', art. cit.

268 'The Evolution of Pastoralism and Indo-European Origin', in George Cardona, Henry M Hoenigswald, & Alfred Seen (eds.), *Indo-European and Indo-Europeans*, op. cit., p. 261.

269 'Proto-Indo-European Culture and Archaeology: Some Critical Remarks', in *JIES*, Autumn 1974, pp. 279–287. Cf. also Andrew Sherratt & Susan Sherratt, 'The Archaeology of Indo-European: An Alternative View', art. cit., pp. 584–595.

tradicted by other evidence or is the result of gross misinterpretation of the cultural history of Eastern, Central and Northern Europe."[270] The critiques apply at the same time to the definition that Marija Gimbutas gave to the 'Kurgan tradition' and to the reality or magnitude of the migrations of which she speaks.

A certain number of archaeologists, notably Russian (Dimitri Yakolevich Telegin, Sulimirski) and German (Alexander Häusler), contest the idea of a continuity of steppe culture from 4400/4300 to 3200/2900 BCE.[271] According to these scholars, the phases that Gimbutas denominates as Kurgan I and Kurgan II form a group clearly distinct from the following stages. This group corresponds in a strict sense to the Stredny Stog II culture on the lower course of the Danube, which goes back to 4500 BCE and the Dnieper-Donetz culture, which is distinctly not a Kurgan culture, whereas the Kurgan III and Kurgan IV phases characterising the Jamna cultural complex (*drevnejamna kultura* and *jamna kultura*) are themselves derived from the Sredny Stog II culture of 3500 BCE, and from analogous sites from the Volga and the Don.[272] Observing that the men of the Sredny Stog culture did not inter their dead under a tumulus, but under cairns, and recalling that inhumation in a flexed position did not appear until stage III, which is at the beginning of the Jamna culture, the same authors contest the assimilation made by Gimbutas among the different forms of funeral rites.[273] They equally underscore the fact that there is no common IE word to designate the pit-tombs and the tumulus to which Gimbutas attached such great importance. Basing themselves on this data and other evidence of a similar nature, some have even cast

---

270 In Search of the Indo-Europeans, op. cit., p. 185.

271 Cf. James P Mallory, 'The Chronology of the Early Kurgan Tradition', in *JIES*, Winter 1975–76, p. 261.

272 Nikolaj J Merpert ('Comments on the Chronology of the Early Kurgan Traditions', in *JIES*, 1977, pp. 373–378) proposes an alternative hypothesis of a polycentric type, which derives the Jamna culture both from the Sredny Stog culture and from the Khvalynsk culture, on the middle Volga.

273 Cf. Alexander Häusler, *Die Gräber der älteren Ockergrabkultur zwischen Ural und Dniepr* (Berlin: Akademie, 1974); *Die Gräber der älteren Ockergrabkultur zwischen Dniepr und Karpaten* (Berlin: Akademie, Berlin 1936).

doubt on the IE character of Kurgan II and especially Kurgan I, asking whether the appearance of tumulus tombs, far from representing a local development, could not be accounted for by an exterior influence.

Gimbutas' assertion, according to which the first bearers of the Kurgan culture were immigrants from the east via the lower basin of the Volga, which imposed itself upon the Dnieper-Donetz and Surski cultures, thus giving birth to Sredny Stog I, has also been disputed. James P Mallory[274] finds it doubtful and asserts chronological arguments against it (Kurgan I is not older than Sredny Stog I), as well as anthropological arguments (the representatives of the Dnieper-Donetz culture are large, mesocephalic, 'Cromagnoids'), while those of Sredny Stog II are slender, dolichocepahic, and narrow-faced).

The data concerning the first wave of expansion of the Kurgan people, its dating, and its magnitude have also been deemed unconvincing. Archaeological evidence attesting to the impact of the cultures of 'Old Europe' is meagre. DY Telegine believes that the culture of Sredny Stog II did not play any role in the IE expansion. David W Anthony[275] himself thinks that Marija Gimbutas exaggerated the magnitude of this first wave towards Hungary and Transylvania. According to him, the influence of the Kurgan people in this region really only makes itself felt with the appearance of the Cernavodă-Baden cultural complex (Kurgan II).

The scale of the two other waves has also been thoroughly disputed. An expansion of the Kurgan people to the west of Tisza, in the Central Hungarian plain, is confirmed neither by archaeology nor anthropology.[276] One study of the distribution of tombs of the Kurgan type shows that we only meet them in one part of northeast Bulgaria, south of the lower course of the Danube. It also turns out that the expansion of a steppe pop-

---

274 'The Chronology of the Early Kurgan Tradition, II', in *JIES*, Winter 1976–77, p. 345.

275 'The Archaeology of Indo-European Origins', art. cit., p. 208.

276 J Nemeskéri & L Szathmáry, 'An Anthropological Evaluation of the Indo-European Problem: The Anthropological and Demographic Transition of the Danube Basin', in S Skomal & Edgar C Polomé (eds.), *Proto-Indo-European: The Archaeology of a Linguistic Problem: Studies in Honor of Marija Gimbutas* (Washington, DC: Institute for the Study of Man, 1987), pp. 88–121.

ulation in the Balkans is accompanied by a series of cultural interactions much more complex than the 'dramatic' scenario which Gimbutas lets us believe.[277] Recalling that we already find tombs with circular tumuli during the Neolithic in the British Isles, and that they have not been explained by 'Kurganisation', English archaeologists JM Coles and AF Harding conclude that the argument of funeral rites is not decisive, and that 'the supposedly derivative groups in Europe [as hypothesised by Gimbutas] are in fact *contemporaneous* with the Pit Graves [of the Kurgans] in south Russia, and not appreciably *later* than them'.[278] David W Anthony[279] also feels that Gimbutas' framework poorly explains the Indo-Europeanisation of Europe to the west and north of the Carpathian basin.

The role of the Kurgan culture in the formation of the Indo-Iranian group, via the intermediary of the Andronovo culture, is by contrast more commonly recognised. If we admit that the documents of Mitanni were written in an archaic, Indo-Aryan form, there is a good chance that the ancestor of this language, common Indo-Iranian, was formed before 2000 BCE. From this perspective, the history of the Indo-Iranian group most certainly proceeds via the Andronovo culture, which according to Anthony W Smith represents 'the most archaic archaeological culture that we can reasonably connect to an IE linguistic group'.[280] In the third millennium, this semi-pastoral culture included diverse regional groups installed between the northern steppes of the Black Sea and the Urals, extending to the Yenisei, passing via Kazakhstan and southwest Siberia. It seems to have developed by 2300 BCE, the date that a material culture of the Petrovka II type emerged on the site of old Surtanda-Botai culture, itself derived from the Jamna cultural complex in around 3000 BCE.

---

277 Cf. I Manzura, E Savva, & L Bogataya, 'East-West Interactions in the Eneolithic and Bronze Age Cultures of the North-West Pontic Region', in *JIES*, Spring–Summer 1995, pp. 1–51.

278 *The Bronze Age in Europe: An Introduction to the Prehistory of Europe c. 2000–700 B.C.* (New York: St. Martin's Press, 1979), p. 7.

279 'The Archaeology of Indo-European Origins', art. cit.

280 Ibid., p. 203.

Because we know that the Russian steppes were inhabited in the seventh millennium BCE by Scythian tribes who spoke an Iranian dialect, the hypothesis of continuity between the Kurgan culture and the Scythians seems plausible. Some authors conclude that the Jamna culture had only ever spoken the ancestral Indo-Iranian language. 'The result of this', writes János Makkay, 'is that the Kurgan culture could not have spread any other dialects in Europe or in Asia than those which derive from Indo-Iranian. This hypothesis is further reinforced by the fact that these Indo-Iranian dialects never appeared in the territories situated west or southwest of the zone in which the Kurgan culture originally formed and expanded.'[281] Far from representing the homeland of the PIE community, the Kurgan culture is therefore only a secondary centre constituted by the ancestors of the Indo-Iranian group, which may also include the Proto-Greeks.

But it is above all the pattern proposed by Marija Gimbutas for the Indo-Europeanisation of Northern Europe that roused the strongest objections. This pattern, we have seen, postulates a transformation of the Funnel Beaker civilisation, due to the extension of the Kurgan people towards the north plain, which would lead to the Globular Amphora civilisation, and then from this to Corded Ware. This 'invasionist' thesis, which explains the Indo-Europeanisation of Northern Europe by a migration from the south or east, and that was already affirmed by Hermann Güntert[282] and Ernst Wahle,[283] is firmly rejected by the researchers who hold to a model of authochthonous development.

It is therefore important to assess the situation of the Corded Ware culture and the two cultures which preceded it: the Globular Amphora culture and the Funnel Beaker culture.

---

281 'A Neolithic Model of Indo-European Prehistory', art. cit., p. 207.

282 *Der Ursprung der Germanen*, op. cit. For Güntert, the Germanic peoples were born from the fusion of a pre-IE agricultural people corresponding to the Megalithic culture, and of a population of IE invaders who were superimposed upon them.

283 *Deutsche Vorzeit*, 2nd ed. (Basel: B. Schwabe & Co., 1952).

From Funnel Beakers to Corded Ware

The Corded Ware civilisation (German *Schnurkeramic*, French *céramique cordée*), also called the battle-axe culture (German *Streitaxt*, French *hache de combat*) in reference to its pottery, and which was decorated by applying cords to wet clay and to the numerous perforated battle-axes found in their tombs, makes its appearance from 3100/3000 BCE and culminates around 2200/1900 BCE. Its IE character is well-established, but its origins remain controversial.[284] Four theses are current: (1) a western origin, from Upper Saxony or Thuringia, between the Rhine and the Vistula (Franz Specht, Alexander Häusler, Ulrich Fischer, K Jazdzewski); (2) an eastern origin, between the basin of the Vistula in Poland and the Dnieper region in western Ukraine (Dmitry Kraynov, Raisa Denisova, Miroslav Buchvaldek); (3) an origin from the steppes and forests of the middle course of the Dnieper (Ivan Artemenko, IK Sveshnikov, VP Tretyakov, Sofia Berezanskaïa, N Bondar); or (4) an origin purely from the steppes (Gustav Rosenberg, PV Glob, Karl Struve, Marija Gimbutas, Aleksandr Bryusov, Valentin Danilenko). In 1955, Struve suggested a division of this culture into two groups, one interring its dead with beakers, and the other with both beakers and amphorae. In1958, Fischer proposed a division into three groups (from Hercynia, the Balto-Rhine, and the steppes of the north Black Sea).

Since the 1960s, we have seen that during its peak (around 2500 BCE), the Corded Ware culture covered a much wider territory than previously thought, extending north and west over Germany and the Netherlands, to southern Scandinavia and Switzerland, and north and east through Poland, Ukraine, Belarus, and the Baltic countries, to central Russia, the middle course of the Dnieper, and the upper course of the Volga.[285] In

---

284 Cf. Miroslav Buchvaldek, 'Corded Pottery Complex in Central Europe', in *JIES*, Autumn–Winter 1980, pp. 393–406.

285 Cf. Rimué Rimantienè & Gintautas Cesnys, 'The Pan-European Corded Ware Horizon (A-Horizon) and the Pamariu (Baltic Coastal) Culture', in Karlene Jones-Bley & Martin E Huld (eds.), *The Indo-Europeanization of Northern Europe*, op. cit., pp. 48–53.

north Germany and in Schleswig-Holstein, its first traces are often associated with the megalithic monuments ('*Hunnenbetten*') and megalithic passage tombs, which were later replaced by individual tombs. In Eastern Europe, where it succeeds the Lengyel culture, it also gives birth to the cultures of the middle course of the Dnieper and to the Fatjanovo culture. In Moravia, it seems to blend with the Baden culture in the basin of the Carpathians.[286] In the Baltic countries it mixes with a local Neolithic population, thereby giving birth to the Pamariu culture (Rzucewo), which we consider to be the principal component of the western Baltic culture, and as the first Baltic population of the future Lithuania.[287] In the south of Central Europe, it appears to have undergone the influence of the Bell Beaker culture (German *Glockenbecher*, French *gobelets campaniformes*), which extends from the Rhine and Danube valleys to the British Isles, France, and the Iberian Peninsula. The mix of the two cultures gives rise, at the end of the third millennium, to the Proto-Únětice culture in the southeast (which will be continued later by the Urnfield culture), and to the Safferstetten in the southwest, both of which signal the beginning of the Bronze Age in this region. For Bernard Sergent, the Bell Beaker culture is a simple 'deviation' from the Corded Ware culture (although the morphotype of the representatives of the two cultures would be very different). It is in the Corded Ware culture that Franz Specht sees the origin of the linguistic superstratum that results from the series of innovations shared by the Germanic, Celtic, Italic, and Balto-Slavic languages.

The Funnel Beaker culture (German *Trichterbecher* or TRB, French *gobelets à entonnoir*) emerges around 4400/4000 BCE, and develops

---

286 Zdzislaw Sochacki ('L'importance de la civilisation de Baden dans la problématique de l'énéolithique européen', in *Etudes indo-européennes*, February 1984, pp. 29–45; 'The Relationship between the Baden Culture and the South-East European Cultures', in *JIES*, Autumn–Winter 1985, pp. 257–268) disputes the interpretation given by Marija Gimbutas of the Baden culture, and feels that the differences between this culture of complex genesis and the cultures of 'Old Europe' clearly outweigh the similarities.

287 Cf. MS Midgley, *TRB Culture: The First Farmers of the North European Plain* (Edinburgh: Edinburgh University Press, 1992).

through to 3500/3400 BCE. Its westernmost group is situated in Belgium and the Netherlands, and its easternmost group in Poland and Ukraine, with other groups covering Schleswig-Holstein, Denmark, Sweden, Mecklenburg, central Germany, Bohemia, and Moravia.[288] Its funerary rites include individual flat graves, as well as megalithic tombs and tumulus graves. Ward H Goodenough directly associates the development of this culture with the distribution of the 'Old European' toponyms and hydronyms identified by Hans Krahe. Alexander Häusler and Lothar Kilian identify it with the PIE community. As with the Corded Ware culture, the origins of the Funnel Beaker culture are controversial. Some archaeologists have derived it from the Lengyel culture and think that it gave rise to the Baden culture as well as the Michelsberg culture along the Rhine, perhaps together with influences stemming from the cultures of Chassey (eastern France), Cerny, and Rössen.[289] For others, to the contrary, it is derived from the Michelberg culture (H Schwabissen), or else it was born in southeast Poland or northwest Ukraine (Carl J Becker, Jan Lichardus). For others still, it is explained by a local acculturation of Neolithic cultures in Central Europe (MP Palmer, Jorgen Jensen), or by an extension of the Dnieper-Donetz culture (Dimitri Y Telegin).

For Carl-Heinz Böttcher,[290] who seems to us to have the most reliable view on the subject, the Funnel Beaker culture was born around 3000 BCE from the fusion, along the course of the Vistula, the Oder, the Elbe, and the Rhine, of the Band Ware culture (German *Bandkeramik*, French *céramique rubanée*), a civilisation formed in the sixth millennium over the middle course of the Danube between lower Austria and west Hungary, and the Ellerbek-Ertebølle culture, a civilisation of seafaring hunter-fishermen whose origins are situated on the banks of the North Sea and the Baltic.

---

288 Cf. Evzen & Jiri Neustupny, *Czechoslovakia before the Slavs* (London: Thames & Hudson, 1961).

289 'La culture des gobelets à entonnoir en Europe centrale: Interprétation de sa genèse et de ses structures sociales', in *Etudes indo-européennes*, 10, 1991, pp. 9–69.

290 Ibid., p. 57.

During the epoch of its greatest extension, the Band Ware culture seems to have dominated the entire central part of the European continent, from the Black Sea Canal and from the north Carpathians to central Germany, Portugal, and western Ukraine. The cultures of Rössen and Lengyel were regional variants. They themselves were the inheritors of the Starčevo culture, which, in the seventh millennium, extended itself into Yugoslavia and over vast sectors of southwest Europe, while having contacts with Anatolia and the Near East. Its bearers then rose northward as weather conditions allowed, around 5000 BCE. As for the Ellerbek-Ertebølle culture, it would issue from the Maglemosian culture, a civilisation of hunter-gatherers and fishermen appearing at the end of the last glacial period on the banks of the North Sea and the Baltic. Around 5000 BCE, natural catastrophes led to the submersion of the Dogger Bank (which until then divided the North Sea into two basins) and brought about the disappearance of the Maglemosian culture. The Ellerbek-Ertebølle culture that would succeed it (Alexander Häusler, Brigitte Hulthen) traded flint, amber, salt, and perhaps also copper from Heligoland.

The cultures of Baalberg-Salzmünde (in central Germany and Bohemia), Altheim, and Michelsberg represent the regional extensions of the Funnel Beaker culture, which also maintained contacts with the megalithic cultures of Ireland, England (Windmill Hill), Brittany, and Iberia, at the same time as with the cultures of Vinča, Baden, and Cucuteni-Tripolye in southeast Europe, the north Black Sea cultures, and even the Sumerian and Predynastic Egyptian cultures. 'Trade and well-being', writes Carl-Heinz Böttcher, 'then reached a flourishing peak, which they had never known before in Central and Southern Europe. It would be recovered and partially surpassed only by the cultures of the Bronze Age, after a significant decline occurring in the intermediate period towards the end of the Cuprolithic'.[291] The first fortified village belonging to the Funnel Beaker

---

291 Ibid., p. 55.

culture was discovered in the 1950s by Edwin Taubert at Büdelsdorf, near Rendsburg in Schleswig-Holstein.[292]

The Globular Amphora culture (German *Kugelamphoren*, French *amphores globulaires*) developed in the second half of the fourth millennium, between 3500/3400 and 3100/3000 BCE, being an intermediate period between the Funnel Beaker culture and the Corded Ware culture. It appears on the north European plain, north of the Carpathians, on the current territory of Germany, Poland, Volyn, and northern Moldavia, and then extends from Denmark to Lithuania.[293] The Polish archaeologist Tadeusz Wislanski[294] places its cradle in the basin of the Oder and the Warta. Its extension over the southeast banks of the Baltic is no doubt connected to the amber trade.[295] We know little about the human type of its representatives, which Olga Necrasov describes as 'proto-Europoid, tempered by some brachycephalisation'. It is the direct ancestor of the Corded Ware culture.

The broader question is to know whether this Globular Amphora culture and the Corded Ware culture which followed it constituted a local extension of the Funnel Beaker culture, of if they resulted from an exterior influence, as was the case with the Kurgan culture.

For Marija Gimbutas, the Globular Amphora culture is born in southern Poland and northwest Ukraine, which constituted the last habitat of the Proto-Slavs, in connection with the second wave of Kurgan expansion.[296] In around 3000 BCE, its representatives head towards Belarus,

---

292 An excavation campaign, undertaken on this site between 1968 and 1974, allowed the remains of more than 13,000 pieces of pottery to be recovered.

293 *Corded Ware and Globular Amphora North-East of the Carpathians* (London: Athlone Press, 1968); and 'Die Kugelamphorenkultur im Flussgebiet der Oder und der Weichsel', in *Zeitschrift für Archäologie*, 1976, pp. 6–11.

294 Cf. Rimué Rimantienè & Gintautas Cesnys, 'The Late Globular Amphora Culture and its Creators in the East Baltic Area from Archaeological and Anthropological Point of View', in *JIES*, Autumn–Winter 1990, pp. 339–358.

295 Alexandre Kosko, 'The Migration of Steppe and Forest-Steppe Communities in Central Europe', in *JIES*, 1990, pp. 309–329.

296 Cf. Marija Gimbutas, 'The Kurgan Wave #2 (c. 3400–3200 B.C.) into Europe and the Following Transformation of Culture', art. cit. Cf. also K Kristiansen, 'Prehistoric Migrations: The Case of the Single Grave and Corded Ware Cultures', in *Journal*

central Russia, the eastern Baltic, Denmark, southern Sweden, Norway, and the Netherlands, which they would successively Indo-Europeanise. This penetration would be further deepened with the Corded Ware culture. To support this thesis, Gimbutas based herself principally on the funerary rites of the Globular Amphora culture, which she described as similar to the steppe culture of Majkop (Mikhajlova stage I), and different from the Funnel Beaker culture, which was characterised by long graves, often placed in megalithic passages or corridors. Marija Gimbutas concluded that the Funnel Beaker culture was not IE, but belonged to the culture which built the megalithic passages; that it had only been Indo-Europeanised late, under the influence of the steppe cultures; and that the Globular Amphora culture was the result of this Indo-Europeanisation.

This thesis is strongly rejected by those (Alexander Häusler, Ulrich Fischer, Evzen Neustupny, Carl Heinz Böttcher, Lothar Kilian, E Sturms, LS Klejn) who see in the Globular Amphora culture an autochthonous development by an eastern group of the Funnel Beaker culture, which, they affirm, already belongs to the IE community. These critics note, along with the majority of archaeologists from eastern countries, that there is no archaeological or anthropological evidence for the migration postulated by Gimbutas. They also emphasise that the Globular Amphora culture and the Corded Ware culture substantially occupied the same territory as the Funnel Beaker culture, which tends to confirm that they are the extension, perhaps by the intermediary of the Baalberg-Salzmünde culture, who had already used tumulus tombs by around 3600 BCE. Lothar Kilian adds, in contrast Gimbutas' assertions, that we already find tumulus tombs in the Funnel Beaker culture. Alexander Häusler[297] points out that the same applies to the ritual inhumations of animals, cited by Gimbutas as proof of steppe culture influence. He mentions, furthermore, that the funer-

---

of *Danish Archaeology*, 1989, pp. 211–225; and Alexandre Kosko, 'The Migration of Steppe and Forest-Steppe Communities in Central Europe', in *JIES*, 1990, pp. 309–329.

297 'Struktur und Evolution der Bestattungssitten im Neolithikum und in der frühere Bronzezeit Mittel- und Osteuropas', in *Etnographisch-Archäologische Zeitschrift*, 1992, pp. 274–296.

ary costumes of the Baden culture differ completely from those of the Kurgans, which rules out the idea that the first could play an intermediary role between the steppe culture and that of the Funnel Beaker culture.

Contrary to Gimbutas' claims, recent research has also shown that the development of Corded Ware culture was barely influenced from the outside.[298] JP Mallory himself recognises that archaeology alone does not confirm the Eastern origin.[299] He adds that 'there is no real proof of an expansion of Jamnaya invaders throughout the north European plain having led to the cultural complex of Corded Ware.'[300] The human type of the inner core of the Corded Ware culture, which is a medium-size type — slender, leptomorphic, and meso-dolichocephalic — no longer correspond to the larger type, more brachycephalic, of the Kurgan culture (which is also that of the Bell Beaker culture). Moreover, this slender type is better represented at the beginning of the Corded Ware culture than in the following stages, which tends to contradict the thesis of an original 'genetic Kurganisaton' (Ilse Schwidetzky).[301] Lothar Kilian again empha-

---

298 Cf. Ulrich Fischer, 'Mitteldeutschland und die Schnurkeramik: Ein kulturhistorischer Versuch', in *Jahresschrift für Mitteldeutsche Vorgeschichte*, 1958, pp. 254–298; MP Palmer, *Jungneolithische Studien*, Lund-Bonn 1962; Evzen Neustupny, 'Economy of the Corded Ware Cultures', in *Archeologické Rozhledy*, 1969, 43–67; Juri Neustupny, 'Archaeological Comments to the Indo-European Problem', in *Origini*, 1976, pp. 7–15; Alexander Häusler, 'Der Ursprung der Schnurkeramik nach Aussage der Grab- und Bestattungssitten', in *Jahresschrift für Mitteldeutsche Vorgeschichte*, 1983, pp. 9–30; K Jazdzewski, *Urgeschichte Mitteleuropas*, Polish Academy Press, Wrocław 1984; Alexander Häusler, 'Kulturbeziehungen zwischen Ost- und Mitteleuropa im Neolithikum?', in *Jahresschrift für Mitteldeutsche Vorgeschichte*, 1985, pp. 21–74; Erika Nagel, *Die Erscheinung der Kugelamphoren-Kultur im Norden der DDR* (Berlin: Akademie, 1985); Hermann Behrens, 'Zur Problemsituation der Mittelelbe-Saale-Schnurkeramik', in *Archäologische Korrespondenzblatt*, 1989, pp. 37–46; and Alexander Häusler, 'Zum Verhältnis von Ockergrabkultur und Schnurkeramik', in *Praehistorica*, 1992, pp. 341–348.

299 *In Search of the Indo-Europeans*, op. cit., pp. 254 & 264.

300 Ibid., p. 246.

301 Cf. Ilse Schwidetzky & FW Rösing, 'The Influence of the Steppe People Based on Physical Anthropological Data in Special Consideration to the Corded-Battle-Axe Culture', art. cit.; and Roland Menk, 'A Synopsis of the Physical Anthropology of the Corded Ware Complex on the Background of the Expansion of the Kurgan Culture', art. cit.

sises the frequent presence of battle-axes and goblets decorated with cords in the tombs of the Corded Ware culture, while we find nothing of the sort during the same period in the tombs of the Kurgans.[302] Häusler concludes that the thesis of Gimbutas 'vividly contradicts' everything we know of Corded Ware culture, and adds that the Kurgan culture, under the form imagined by Gimbutas, 'has never existed'.[303]

It is therefore necessary to assume a very long continuity of IE presence in north Germany, corresponding to the lineage: Maglemose > Ellerbek-Ertebølle > Funnel Beaker > Globular Amphora > Corded Ware. An analogous development had already been proposed by Oscar Montelius[304] at the end of the nineteenth century. From this perspective, the pre-IE substratum was represented by the culture of megalith builders, and perhaps also (but this point is highly debated) by the Band Ware culture. The Indo-Europeanisation of Scandinavia would occur in the third millennium, during the epoch of Corded Ware culture.

The continuity would be equally strong between the Corded Ware culture and the first culture commonly recognised as Germanic: the Jastorf culture of the sixth century BCE. Archaeology indeed shows that northern Europe had not known any significant alteration of its people from the late Neolithic to the Iron Age. The advent of the Nordic Bronze Age, which extends from around 1700 BCE until the middle of the first millennium, results from a local evolution. The development of trade relations with the south (amber, furs, smoked fish, grains, livestock), particularly significant in this epoch, does not seem to have brought any notable population change.[305] The only major cultural innovation is the

---

302 We find the same observation in Homer L Thomas, 'The Indo-European Problem: Complexities of the Archaeological Evidence', in *JIES*, Spring–Summer 1992, p. 13.

303 *Kratylos*, 1991, pp. 96 & 98.

304 *Die Chronologie der ältesten Bronzezeit in Norddeutschland und Skandinavien*, 4th ed., Braunschweig 1900.

305 Cf. Edgar C Polomé, 'Methodological Approaches to the Ethno- and Glottogenesis of the Germanic People', in P Sture Ureland (ed.), *Entstehung von Sprachen und Völkern: Glotto- und ethnogenetische Aspekte europäischer Sprachen* (Tübingen: Max Niemeyer, 1985), pp. 46–49.

transition from inhumation to cremation as the dominant funeral rite. The end of the Bronze Age also suggests a gradual transition to the metallurgy of iron, mastery of which the Germanic people probably acquired via the intermediary of the Celts.[306] From this date, the mastery of iron metallurgy meant that the Northern Europeans no longer depended on the south for the importation of the metal. This independence probably favoured the emergence of a distinct culture, as testified by the rapid expansion of the Jastorf culture. Born between Denmark and the mouth of the Oder, this culture dominated northern Europe during the Iron Age, and at its height, its centre was situated by the central and lower course of the Elbe, extending over Schleswig-Holstein, Lower Saxony, western Pomerania, western Mecklenburg, and Brandenburg, stretching west via the Harpstedt culture.[307]

Such facts suggest that the Germanic languages represent the outcome of a long process of maturation for an IE idiom present in northern Europe since the Neolithic. The question remains open, however, of whether the representatives of the Corded Ware culture (or the Funnel Beaker culture) used a Proto-Germanic language, or whether they used a common language corresponding to the 'Old European' of Krahe or the 'Northwest Indo-European' of Meillet. According to Jean-Paul Allard, it cannot be ruled out that the Germanic peoples had been 'the product of an amalgam in which a conquering and invading Indo-European element entered the diverse autochthonous elements which existed prior to the Indo-European expansion, and to which prehistorians have given, for better or worse, the name of megalithic people.'[308] The same hypothesis has been sustained by Hermann Güntert[309] and Jan de Vries.[310] However,

---

306 The name for 'iron' in common Germanic, *i:sarna-, possibly derives from Celtic.

307 Cf. Gustav Schwantes, 'Die Jastorf-Zivilisation', in *Festschrift für Paul Reinecke zum 75. Geburtstag*, Mainz 1950; and Herbert Schutz, *The Prehistory of Germanic Europe* (New Haven, CT: Yale University Press, 1983), p. 310.

308 'La royauté wotanique des Germains, II', in *Etudes indo-européennes*, April 1982, pp. 31–32.

309 *Der Ursprung der Germanen*, op. cit.

310 *Die geistige Welt der Germanen*, 1964.

the importance of the pre-IE linguistic substratum in the Germanic languages has ceased to be debated. According to some authors (Güntert,
Scardigli), consonantal mutation (*Lautverschiebung*) in Germanic is better explained by the presence of such a substrate, but this hypothesis raises
serious chronological problems.[311] Criticism of the notion of a substrate in
Germanic has already been made by Julius Pokorny,[312] according to whom
nothing exists in the Germanic proto-language that we can compare, for
example, to the Finno-Ugrian substrate in the language of the Balto-Slavs.
This critique has been taken up and accentuated by Günther Neumann.[313]
The study of the vocabulary, morphology, phonology, and syntax does
not allow us to identify a greater divergence in relation to PIE in the
Germanic languages than in the other languages.[314] As for the lexicon, the
statistical data gathered by Norman Bird[315] also shows that 67 per cent of
the Germanic vocabulary is of IE origin, against 60 per cent for Greek, 54
per cent for the Baltic languages, and 50 per cent for Vedic Sanskrit.

The Germanic languages seem to have been particularly close to the
origin of the Italic languages. It is only after the departure of the two
migratory waves to the south, which, during the epoch of the Urnfield
culture, led to the Villanovan (the Pianello-Timmari complex) and the
Terramare culture from 1100/1000 BCE, that the relations between the
Germanic languages and the Celtic languages became tighter.[316] The Celtic

---

311   This mutation, which led to the transformation of '*k*' into '*h*', is generally dated to
      around 500 BCE. It is this dating which allows us to attribute a distinct linguistic
      identity to the Jastorf culture. Cf. Richard Schrodt, *Die germanische Lautverschiebung
      und ihre Stellung im Kreise der indogermanischen Sprachen*, 2nd ed. (Vienna: Karl M
      Halosar, 1976), pp. 59–72.

312   'Substrattheorie und Urheimat der Indogermanen', in *Mitteilungen der
      Anthropologischen Gesellschaft in Wien*, 1936, pp. 69–91.

313   *Substrate im Germanischen?*, op. cit.

314   Cf. Winfred P Lehmann, *Proto-Indo-European Phonology* (Austin: University of
      Texas Press, 1952).

315   *The Distribution of Indo-European Root Morphemes: A Checklist for Philologists*, op.
      cit. He specifies, however, that the results were obtained on the basis of reconstruc-
      tions and etymological links proposed in 1959 by Julius Pokorny.

316   Cf. Ernst Schwarz, *Germanische Stammeskunde* (Heidelberg: Carl Winter, 1956);
      Edgar C Polomé, 'Who Are the Germanic People?', in Susan Nacev Skomal & EC

and Germanic peoples then seem to have entered into prolonged contact, and during the course of this, the latter borrowed much form the former, notably from the technical domain and the military arts. According to Norman Bird, Germanic and Celtic share 674 lexical correspondences with the other IE languages, a figure which can be raised to 703 if we include strict Celto-Germanic isoglosses, almost as many as the number of Balto-Slavic correspondences (715). It is also during this period that the Celts, whose presence would extend from Spain and the British Isles to the Balkans and Asia Minor, would become the most important western IE group. However, contrary to what has sometimes been asserted, there are no attested traces of a Celtic presence in the central territory of the Germanic area proper: between the Elbe and the Weser, and to the north beyond the Elbe.

Palaeolithic and Mesolithic

If the Globular Amphora and the Corded Ware cultures do not derive from that of the Kurgans, the question then arises of how they were Indo-Europeanised. The most plausible answer is that the Funnel Beaker culture was clearly already IE. Alexander Häusler, who identifies this culture with the homeland, concludes that we must invert the direction of the migration postulated by Gimbutas. From this point of view, it is the Kurgan culture which could have undergone the influence of the Funnel Beaker culture. The Kurgan culture would not have either the importance or extent attributed to it by Gimbutas, and it would only truly begin with the Jamnaya culture, around 3500 BCE. This was already the opinion of Carl Schuchhardt,[317] for whom the model of the tumulus grave was born not in the milieu of the steppes, but in Northern Europe. The Corded Ware people were then diffused in three directions: towards the north, in the

---

Polomé (eds.), *Proto-Indo-European: The Archaeology of a Linguistic Problem*, op. cit., pp. 216–244; and Edgar C Polomé, 'Sir William Jones and the Position of Germanic', in *JIES*, 1988, pp. 209–232.

317 *Alteuropa: Die Entwicklung seiner Kulturen und Völker* (Berlin: Walter de Gruyter, 1944).

midst of the megalithic cultures; towards the south; and towards the east. However, there is no clear archaeological evidence of such an influence. All that we can note is that the beginning of the Funnel Beaker culture co-incides with Kurgan I in the classification of Gimbutas. The Corded Ware culture is also contemporary with the end of the Jamna cultural horizon, an epoch during which both cultures bordered each other in Galicia and along the Slovenian Carpathians between south Poland and Hungary.

It is clear that no solution to the problem of the homeland can be considered convincing unless it simultaneously explains both the origin of the Kurgan tradition and that of the Corded Ware culture. If the IE cultures of Northern Europe did not derive from those of the steppes, and if the reverse derivation is no longer possible, there is no other alternative than for both of them to come from the same, common culture. Taking the chronology into account, the homeland must then be sought in the Mesolithic, which in Europe lasts from 9000 to 6000 BCE, or even in the Palaeolithic, that is to say around 9000/10000 BCE. This hypothesis is not new. From 1925, Paul Kretschmer[318] felt that it was necessary to seek the primitive habitat of the IE in an epoch much more remote than previously thought. In 1932, Herbert Kühn[319] proposed to place the homeland in the Upper Palaeolithic, and assimilated the PIE to the Magdalenians. The idea of a PIE community dating back to the Palaeolithic was taken up by Seger in 1936, by Gustav Schwantes in 1958, and by Vladimir Georgiev in the 1960s. Homer L Thomas[320] emphasises for his part that, contrary to what

318   *Die indogermanische Sprachwissenschaft. Eine Einführung für die Schule* (Göttingen: Vandenhoeck & Ruprecht, 1925).

319   'Herkunft und Heimat der Indogermanen', in *Proceedings of the First International Congress of Prehistoric and Protohistoric Sciences, London, 1932* (London: Oxford University Press & Humphrey Milford, 1934), pp. 237–242.

320   'Indo-European: From the Paleolithic to the Neolithic', in Mohammad Ali Jazayery (ed.), *Perspectives on Indo-European Language, Culture and Religion: Studies in Honor of Edgar C Polomé*, op. cit., vol. 1, pp. 12–37. Cf. also Homer L Thomas, 'Archaeological Evidence for the Migrations of the Indo-Europeans', in Edgar C Polomé (ed.), *The Indo-Europeans in the Fourth and Third Millenia* op. cit.; and 'The Indo-European Problem: Complexities of the Archaeological Evidence', in *JIES*, Spring–Summer 1992, p. 20.

we often thought, the transition from the Neolithic to the Palaeolithic was made without breaking the continuity, so there is nothing to stop us from seeking the homeland in the Mesolithic. Tadeus Sulmirski[321] affirms that we cannot reject *a priori* the hypothesis of a Mesolithic origin of the PIE, with some IE language already differentiated at the beginning of the Neolithic. János Makkay[322] also suggests that a large IE linguistic continuum formed very early, with an initial dispersion in the seventh millennium, if not earlier.

Cicerone Poghirc observes that a number of tools for very different purposes (axe, knife, nail, needle, drill, anvil, hammer, javelin, etc.) have a name derived from the PIE root *ak- in the IE languages, which originally designates 'stone'. As this root also signifies 'sharp, piercing, cutting', it clearly deals with stone carved from flint of the Palaeolithic kind, and not polished Neolithic stone. And we also note the absence of a common terminology for pottery. Poghirc concludes that the Neolithic is not the epoch in which the PIE community was formed, but was rather its end, and that the original homeland corresponded in all likelihood to a shifting region of hunter-gatherers who gradually moved as the glaciers retreated at the end of the last ice age. 'In our opinion', he writes, 'the only period that would have favoured the formation of a large community (even if originally small), is by necessity that of a very mobile society, engaged in a permanent process of biological and linguistic crossings, such as the hunter-gatherer-fishermen that correspond approximately to the Lower Palaeolithic and the Mesolithic (...) The end of the glacial periods, followed by the spreading of vegetation and animals proper to historical Europe constitutes, for us, a *terminus post quem*[323] for the presence of Indo-Europeans *in statu nascendi*.[324] This process seems to reflect itself above all

---

321 *Corded Ware and Globular Amphora North-East of the Carpathians*, op. cit.

322 'New Aspects of the PIE and the PU/PFU Homelands', in L Keresztes & S Maticsik (eds.), *Congressus Septimus Internationalis Fenno-Ugristarum*, Debrecen 1990, pp. 55–83; and 'A Neolithic Model of Indo-European Prehistory', art. cit., pp. 193–238.

323 Latin: 'the earliest possible date'. — Ed.

324 Latin: 'in the nascent state'. — Ed.

in the common Indo-European denominations for trees: the attestation of these denominations is more general for the species that spread in Europe between 8000 and 5000 BCE than for those which spread after this date. Also significant is the fact that the names of wild animals (wolf, fox, bear, beaver, etc.) are generally more widespread, even in Indo-Iranian, than the names of domestic animals (...) The Neolithic, which we retained without much reason as the period of the Indo-European community, cannot be accepted. The generalisation of agriculture that occurs during this period requires an attachment to the land and partition into small groups unbound by a central power or a major common interest. Far from favouring unification, such a society by contrast produces linguistic differentiation, the formation of very distinct dialects and languages, as we have demonstrated for the agricultural people of the historical period. Nomadic pastoralism, for which some specialists have made an extensive case, does not lead to unification on a grand scale, as attested for example by the (pre)history of the Iranian tribes. Only a transhumant, or more precisely 'oscillating', pastoralism (always between the same mountains and the same plain) associated with a stable agriculture produces a strong unification, but only within more restricted territories'.[325]

For Lothar Kilian,[326] the IE had already occupied Central and Eastern Europe since the Mesolithic. There is therefore no need to invoke the migrations of subsequent peoples to explain their presence in this region. Kilian postulates a vast original homeland, stretching from the Mesolithic over a space of 2000 to 3000 kilometres, delimited by the North Sea, Baltic, Rhine, Danube, Vistula, and the north of the Black Sea through to the Urals and the Volga. PIE would be differentiated from a more remote stem, from which the Finno-Ugric languages also proceed, between 15000 and 10000 BCE. The IE community would be maintained until around 5000/4500 BCE, before giving birth both to the Funnel Beaker culture and the Kurgans, as well as the Band Ware culture. According to

---

325 'Pour une concordance fonctionnelle et chronologique entre linguistique, archéologie et anthropologie dans le domaine indo-européen', art. cit., pp. 329–330.

326 *Zum Ursprung der Indogermanen*, op. cit.

Alexander Häusler and Carl-Heinz Böttcher, this is the territory upon which Hans Krahe and Wolfgang P Schmid observed the presence of 'Old European' hydronyms, between the Rhine and the Urals, a region that has been Indo-Europeanised since at least the Mesolithic, and where the first individual IE cultures developed. János Makkay, for his part, traces the Northwest IE dialects to the Band Ware culture, from which the Funnel Beaker culture would result. He suggests that the northernmost part of the Funnel Beaker culture, in an area ranging from the estuaries of the Elbe and the Weser to that of the Elbe proper, is the origin of the Proto-Baltic and Proto-Germanic peoples.

These views are congruent with the general movement that has progressively led researchers to situate the PIE much earlier in time than we had previously thought. Whether the discovery of Hittite and Tocharian; the deciphering of Linear B; the attribution of a redaction date to the first Vedic hymns that is much more remote than we thought; evidence for the archaism of certain languages; the hypothesis according to which we must assume an uninflected phase of the common language; the identification of a great divergence in structure between the Anatolian languages on one hand, and Greek and Sanskrit on the other; and finally, quite simply, the new datings furnished by C-14 — numerous indeed is the data that increasingly compels us to abandon the short chronologies and to push the formation and dispersion of the PIE community back into a more distant epoch.

One such solution, however, raises a certain number of objections of an essentially linguistic order. Principal among these objections is that an original homeland as extensive and vast as that envisaged by Kilian or Häusler is incompatible with the formation of a language that is as unitary and homogenous as PIE: in such a hypothesis, linguistic palaeontology would inevitably reveal dialectical differences in the reconstructed language. In regards to this idea, Paul Thieme[327] has already insisted that the

---

327 *Die Urheimat der indogermanischen Grundsprachen* (Mainz: Akademie der Wissenschaften und der Literatur & Wiesbaden: Mainz & Franz Steiner, 1953), p. 28.

common IE language could only have formed on a territory of relatively limited dimensions. More recently, James P Mallory[328] observed that even today, no European language exists whose speakers occupy an immense territory (with the exception of Russia). According to him, the IE could only have formed and above all maintained themselves upon a territory of 250,000 to 500,000 square kilometres.

The other objection concerns the common vocabulary. If we place the dispersion of the IE community too early, the presence in the lexicon of certain common IE words becomes inexplicable. Jean Haudry[329] recalls that, in the fifth millennium, Northern Europe knew neither copper nor the domestic horse, for which, however, we possess common words (*ek-wos-, *áyes-e/os-). This prevents us from dating the final habitat beyond the Cuprolithic. James P Mallory[330] also feels that we cannot seek the original homeland beyond the fifth millennium, taking into account the common words for 'horse' and 'chariot'. The IE also practiced pig breeding (*sû-, *porko-), which is not attested before the Neolithic. Finally, the type of society that we have restored for common IE, with its formulas and its inherited narrative patterns, does not correspond to the Mesolithic, where the only kind of social organisation seems to have been the band (German *Bund*, French *bande*).[331]

It is this which brings James P Mallory to write, 'We can accept a homeland in the region of the Black Sea and the Caspian Sea, although not the least archaeological data exists which allows us to explain the presence of Indo-Europeans in Northern or Central Europe. Otherwise, we can opt for a more extended homeland, situated in the Mesolithic or Palaeolithic between the Rhine and the Volga. However, this solution, which by definition resolves all the archaeological problems, is linguisti-

---

328 Op. cit.

329 'L'origine des Indo-Européens', in *Nouvelle Ecole*, July 1985, pp. 127–128; and 'A pro-pos d'un livre récent', art. cit., p. 212.

330 'Time, Perspective and Proto-Indo-European Culture', in *World Archaeology*, 1976, pp. 44–56.

331 Cf. S Milisauskas, *European Prehistory* (New York: Academic Press, 1978), p. 30.

PALAEOLITHIC AND MESOLITHIC

cally improbable'.[332] We have a choice, in other words, between a model that disagrees with archaeology and a model that is linguistically dubious.

The objections that we have just explained, however, are not so nullifying if we admit that the homeland is not necessarily identical to the last common habitat. The last common habitat may well have been situated in the Cuprolithic, across a relatively vast territory, whereas the first PIE community would have been formed by the Mesolithic, perhaps indeed the Palaeolithic, over a limited territory. What is more, we cannot entirely exclude the possibility of parallel innovations, nor of contacts between already differentiated languages.

Jean Haudry himself has stressed many times that the common habitat that preceded the first dispersion of the PIE community does not necessarily correspond to the place where the *ethnos* (ethnic group) was formed. The idea that it is necessary to distinguish between a 'primary homeland' and a 'secondary homeland' was already advanced at the beginning of the twentieth century by Matthaeus Much[333] and Otto Schreider.[334] Wolfgang Dressler also considers it necessary to distinguish the 'germ cells' (*Keimzelle*) which saw the formation of the PIE language from the problem of the last common homeland before the dispersion. Cicerone Poghirc writes, 'Both the *Schnurkeramik* and the *Bandkeramik*, the Kurgan culture and the Central European Neolithic culture, belong to the Indo-Europeans (...) The great expansion from east to west at the end of the Neolithic and the beginning of the Bronze Age is not '*die erste indogermanische Wanderung*',[335] but one migration after many others'.[336]

---

332 *In Search of the Indo-Europeans*, op. cit., p. 257.

333 *Die Heimat der Indogermanen im lichte der urgeschichtlichen Forschung* (Berlin: Hermann Costenoble, 1902), p. 3.

334 *Die Indogermanen* (Leipzig: Quelle & Mayer, 1911), pp. 160 & 515.

335 'The first Indo-Germanic migration.' — Tr.

336 Art. cit., pp. 331–332.

A Circumpolar Habitat

As to the location where the *ethnos* was formed, it is difficult to ignore the tradition, notably religious, that insistently situates the origin of the PIE peoples and cultures in the 'extreme North'.[337] India and Iran, like the Celtic world, seem to have effectively retained the memory of an Arctic or circumpolar habitat, regularly designated by expressions such as 'islands at the north of the world', the 'abode of the blessed', the 'lands of the gods', the 'lands of the Hyperboreans', the 'lands of the long night', and so on. The Vedic Indians considered the north as 'the abode of the gods' (*Deva-Loka*) and the south as the 'dwelling-place of demons' (*Yama-Loka*). Other myths grant the pole star an essential place in the IE world. In the Classical epoch, a great number of authors (Aeschylus, Pindar, Herodotus, Callimachus, Apollonius of Rhodes, Pausanias, Diodorus of Sicily, Virgil, Strabo, Pliny the Elder, Pomponius Mela, Iamblichus, Aristeas of Proconnesus, etc.) evoke an original homeland for their culture in the northern zones (Thule, Hyperborea).[338] In the fourth century BCE, Pytheas, a seafarer from Marseilles,[339] even strove to rediscover this region. The fragments of his logbook that have come down to us suggest that he went to the Arctic Circle.[340]

Such facts can obviously be explained by considerations linked to 'cosmic symbolism', and this is indeed the most frequent explana-

---

337 Cf. Jean Haudry, 'Linguistique et tradition indo-européenne', in *Nouvelle Ecole*, hiver 1988–89, pp. 116–129 (Spanish trans.: 'Lingüística y tradición indoeuropea', in *Hesperides*, Spring 1996, pp. 437–459).

338 Cf. especially Maria Raffella Calabrese de Feo, 'Gli Iperborei in Pindaro', in Laurent Dubois (ed.), *Poésie et lyrique antiques* (Villeneuve d'Ascq: Presses universitaires du Septentrion, 1995), pp. 97–118.

339 Pytheas was a Greek explorer who circumnavigated modern-day Great Britain and was the first to describe the Arctic region, the Midnight Sun, and the Germanic tribes. — Ed.

340 In 306 CE, the Emperor Constantius Chlorus was still searching north of Great Britain for the region of the world 'where the Sun does not set'. In the twelfth century, Robert Wace, to whom we owe the *Roman de Brut* and *Vie de Merlin l'enchanteur*, encapsulated in two verses the 'hyperborean mystery': '*En North alum, de north venum, / En north fumes nez, en north manum*'.

tion. However, in the eighteenth century, French missionaries brought some astronomical tables back from India which were deposited in the Royal Library. They were studied by the astronomer Jean-Sylvain Baily (1736–1793), who demonstrated that these tables were incorrect for the latitude of India, but agreed very precisely with a septentrional latitude of 49 degrees north. Baily drew the conclusion that it was in this latitude that 'different languages have been born from the maternal and primitive language'. A century later, the Indian Lokamanya Bāl Gangādhar Tilak (1856–1920)[341] came to even more radical conclusions, basing himself on the study of a certain number of treatises and Vedic rituals, notably the *Devayana* and the *Pitriyana*, which entailed a division of the year into two parts, one dark and the other light, as in the polar regions where only one 'day' and one 'night' is known, each six months long. This Vedic and Iranian homology between the day and the year,[342] which is only understood if the latter includes six months of darkness and six months of light separated by one or more 'dawns', corresponds to the homology between the Germanic name for 'day', *dagaz-* (German *Tag*, English *day*), and the Lithuanian name for 'summer', *dâgas*. The Avesta likewise relates that, in the original country of the Aryas, winter lasted six months, whereas summer only lasted two (*Vendidad*, 1.3–4, 2.20). To develop this thesis, Tilak made further appeal to numerous Greek, Roman, Slavic, Avestan, and Indian myths all evoking a circumpolar abode characterised by an endless night. He deduced that the contents of the Vedas were much older than their transcription, that the authors of these books were men of prehis-

---

341 *Orion, or Researches into the Antiquity of the Vedas* (Bombay: Mrs Radhabhai Atmaram Sagoon, 1893); and *The Arctic Home in the Vedas, Being also a New Key to the Interpretation of Many Vedic Texts and Legends* (London: Arktos, 2011). James P Mallory, who regards the theory of Tilak as 'incredible', nevertheless believes that it represents 'the culmination of an extremely long tradition of analysis of Indo-Aryan myth' (*In Search of the Indo-Europeans*, op. cit., p. 277). [Tilak (1856–1920), in addition to being a scholar, was also the founder of the Indian Independence Movement which ultimately led to India being freed from British colonisation, and he is also considered one of the founding fathers of modern India. — Ed.]

342 Vide:vda:t (Vendi:da:d), 2.41: 'They consider (*man*) as a day (*ayar*) that which is a year (*ya:r*)'.

tory and foreign to the Indian subcontinent, and that the PIE people must have had their primitive habitat in a location which today corresponds to the pole, or to a region close to the pole, a region from which they were driven by a cataclysm corresponding to the last glacial period (Würm IV: 12000–9000 BCE).

GM Bongard-Levin and EA Grantovskij[343] also believe that the Indo-Aryans, Iranians, and Scythians refer to a common mythological heritage in which the north occupies a primordial place. Their thesis attributes an extended stay in western Siberia to the ancestors of the Indo-Iranian group, during which they would have been in contact with the 'peoples of the Taiga'. Most of them would have then emigrated towards Transoxiana and Bactria, then towards the Indo-Gangetic Plain and Iran, whereas those who stayed behind would constitute the Scythians. In his book on Stonehenge, Gerald S Hawkins[344] asserts that for his part the theses of Tilak are 'astronomically valid'. The prehistorian Frank Bourdier believes that the IE languages 'had been originally spoken by a people who were active in the circumpolar regions, using a hierarchical organisation for rearing and hunting'. Christian J Guyonvarc'h and Françoise Le Roux write, 'The events of the greatest consequence for the history of humanity are produced outside the accessible limits of history itself. There are perhaps four or five millennia when conquering masses speaking all the related languages abandoned, for reasons which we will never know, a region north of Eurasia, which is preferable not to locate on a map with too great precision. We recognise that a memory remains of this *arctic habitat*[345] in the conception of the northern origin of the Irish *Túatha dé Dánann* and, in another form, in the name of the Hyperboreans, which the Greeks used to designate the Celts (or the Germanic peoples) of northwest Europe'.[346]

---

343 *De la Scythie à l'Inde: Enigmes de l'histoire des anciens Aryens* (Paris: Institut d'études iraniennes de l'Université de l'Sorbonne nouvelle, 1974) (2nd ed.: Klincksieck, 1981).

344 *Stonehenge Decoded* (Garden City, NY: Doubleday, 1965).

345 Emphasis ours.

346 *La civilisation celtique*, op. cit., p. 16. Cf. also the interview with Christian J Guyonvarc'h published in *Antaios*, 8/9, 1995.

This thesis of a primaeval circumpolar habitat is obviously connected with what we know of the last glacial period.[347] The Würm glaciation began from 70,000 BCE. The late glacial period (Würm III and IV), which is near the end, coincides with the beginning of the Holocene, between 12000 and 9000 BCE. A human presence is also attested in the north from around 15000 BCE (the cultures of Stellmoor and Klosterhund in Denmark, of Fosna and Komsa in Norway, and of Backastog in Sweden), before the melting of the glaciers, which would flourish in Denmark with the Kongemose culture. The Pas-de-Calais[348] will only open around 7000 BCE. The warming of the climate occurs from this date, and combined with the subsequent diffusion of agriculture, is necessarily translated into population growth and the settlement of previously unoccupied territories.

The causes of glaciations, like the periods of warming which follow them, are not always known. In addition to theories that link glacial cycles to the position of the Earth relative to the Sun, we find others which appeal to massive catastrophes (earthquakes, volcanic eruptions, flooding) caused by the passage of a celestial body (a comet?) through the Earth's atmosphere. Such an event is likely to produce a modification of the Earth's

---

347 The assertion by Bernard Sergent that 'the polar or sub-polar origin of the "Aryans" is a theory appearing in Germany's Nazi writings (the "glacial" theory of Hörbiger)' ('Penser — et mal penser — les Indo-Européens', art. cit., p. 675) seems particularly unwarranted. The observations of Bailly date from the end of the eighteenth century, the works of Tilak from 1903. The book by Georg Biedenkapp (*Der Nordpol als Völkerheimat* Jena: H Costenoble) on the same theme is from 1906. As for the extravagant theory of Hörbiger, '*Glazialkosmologie*' or '*Welteislehre*', it emerges in 1894 and was the object of a systematic development between 1905 and 1912 (Philipp Fauth, *Hörbigers Glacial-Kosmogonie: Eine neue Entwickelungsgeschichte des Weltalls und des Sonnensystems* [Kaiserslautern: Hermann Kayser, 1913]). Hörbiger, born in 1860, died in 1932. Neither in his writings nor those of his disciples (Hans Wolfgang Behn, Georg Hinzpeter, Hanns Fischer, Gerhardt Giehm, Philipp Fauth, H Voigt, etc.), nor in the journal *Der Schlüssel zum Weltgeschehen*, published by this circle from 1925, do we find the least allusion to a 'polar or subpolar origin' of the IE. Cf. on this subject Brigitte Nagel, *Die Welteislehre* (Stuttgart: Verlag für Geschichte der Naturwissenschaften und der Technik, 1991). We may add that to our knowledge, no book published in Germany between 1933 and 1945 has ever defended, nor even merely evoked, the hypothesis of a circumpolar habitat of the PIE.

348 One of the northernmost provinces of France, along the North Sea coast. — Ed.

angle of inclination relative to its orbit, thus shifting the poles. It cannot be excluded that regions which were once temperate would find themselves suddenly covered by glaciers. Most of the IE traditions (of which we find equivalents in other traditions, particularly Oriental and American Indian) seem to have preserved the memory of cosmic catastrophes of this kind, which are regularly linked with the irruption of a 'great winter' or a 'cosmic night': *Ragnarök*, 'fate of the gods', and *Fimbulvetr*, 'cosmic winter' in the Germano-Scandinavian tradition; in the Indo-Iranian world, Yama (Yima) survives this winter by interring himself in the *vara*, 'enclosure'.[349] What we have here may be a dramatised representation of the initial cosmology or of the final eschatology, but these traditions may also refer to real events. Furthermore, as we have seen, it is certainly during the last glaciation that the phenomenon of depigmentation occurred, which led to the emergence of the blond type. For all these reasons, and despite the necessarily speculative character of such a hypothesis, we cannot exclude the idea *a priori* that the primaeval IE habitat was situated in a circumpolar region, which could well have been temperate prior to the glaciation.

Provisional Conclusions

At the end of this investigation, which has surveyed a particularly complex range of data, we can only conclude with caution. The problem of the IE homeland remains unsolved to this day. At the very least, the existing research has allowed us to eliminate untenable hypotheses. The solution advanced by Colin Renfrew is obviously one of those which cannot be seriously retained. That of Marija Gimbutas is more coherent, for there can be no doubt that the steppe cultures of the Jamna type, despite the chronology and scale attributed to them, played a role in the IE expansion. However, it is less convincing for explaining the Indo-Europeanisation of Central and Northern Europe, and the formation of the 'northwest group'.

---

349   Cf. Jean Haudry, 'Traverser l'eau de la ténèbre hivernale', in *Etudes indo-européennes*, June 1985; and 'Les Rbhus et les Alfes', in *Bulletin d'études indiennes*, 5, 1987, p. 207.

The thesis of a final common habitat, from which both the Funnel Beaker culture and the steppe culture of the Jamna type would proceed, appears the most likely to be true. The double Pontic/Nordic source results from an initial separation of the northwest and southeast group occurring in the fifth millennium, that is, at the beginning of stage II of PIE (*mittelindogermanisch*). The Anatolian branch had been the first to separate from the common trunk. The Tocharian branch would represent an early scission from the northwest group. The Funnel Beaker culture, continued by the Globular Amphora and Corded Ware cultures, would result in the Germanic, Celtic, and Italic proto-languages; from the Kurgan culture, the Indo-Iranian, Mycenaean-Greek, and Armenian cultures would arise. Concerning the last common habitat, which should be pushed back at least to the Mesolithic, there is much evidence to situate it in the Baltic sector, which is the only place where the IE appear truly autochthonous. The inquiry into hydronyms conducted by Hans Krahe points in this direction, as does the fact that the Baltic languages seem to contain practically no pre-IE substratum.[350] The Baltic and Slavic proto-languages would have developed directly from those of the common habitat, in likely relation with those of the northwest. This solution is close to that sustained by Alexander Häusler and Lothar Kilian, but is distinguished by the fact that it does not identify the homeland with the vast Indo-Europeanised zone which they postulate in Central and Eastern Europe, the Baltic countries, and the Caspian. They give a certain coherence to the hypothesis of a primordial circumpolar habitat, situated north of the Baltic countries in the period of the last glaciation, and the depigmentation produced during this epoch would also explain the presence of the blond type among the IE. It is not irreconcilable, therefore, with a more distant common linguistic stem, from which both the PIE languages and the Finno-Ugric languages would be derived.

---

350 Cf. Wolfgang P Schmid, 'Baltische Gewässernamen und das vorgeschichtliche Europa', art. cit.; 'Baltisch und Indogermanisch', in *Baltistica*, 1976, pp. 115–122; and *Indogermanistische Modelle und osteuropäische Frühgeschichte* (Mainz: Akademie der Wissenschaften und der Literatur & Wiesbaden: Franz Steiner, 1978).

Four Final Remarks

1. Georges Dumézil and Indo-European Studies

Georges Dumézil, as we have seen above, is never truly concerned with the question of the original homeland. Of essential relevance to linguistics and archaeology, this question escapes his speciality: the comparative history of religions. The criticisms which have been addressed to him by researchers who do not share his views, and with whom he was engaged in polemics for the entirety of his life, no longer bear on this subject.[351] But it is above all for methodological reasons that Dumézil could hardly approach this problem. The ahistorical, 'structural' perspective in which he situates himself effectively prevents him from placing the object of his work in chronological history or precise protohistory. Dumézil, in other words, is never concerned to inscribe the mental and politico-religious structures that he studies in real time. It is not impossible that this ap-

---

351 The principles of these critiques emanate from Indologists such as Paul Thieme (*Mitra and Aryaman* [New Haven, CT: Transactions of the Connecticut Academy of Arts and Sciences, 1957), Jan Gonda (*Triads in the Veda* [Amsrerdam: North-Holland, 1976), and I Gershevitch; from Classicists such as André Piganiol, HH Rose, and John Brough ('The Tripartite Ideology of the Indo-Europeans: An Experiment in Method', in *Bulletin of the School of Oriental and African Studies*, 1959, pp. 69–85); and from Germanists such as R Derolez (*De godsdienst der Germanen*, Roermond & Maaseik, 1959), Karl Helm ('Mythologie auf alten und neuen Wegen', in *Beiträge zur Geschichte der deutschen Sprache und Literatur*, 1955, pp. 333–365), Ernst Alfred Philippson ('Die Genealogie der Götter in germanischer Religion, Mythologie und Theologie', in *Illinois Studies in Language and Literature*, 1953, 3; 'Phänomenologie, vergleichende Mythologie und germanische Religionsgeschichte', in *Publications of the Modern Language Association*, 1962, pp. 187–193), and RI Page ('Dumézil Revisited', in *Saga-Book*, XX, 1978–79, pp. 49–69). Cf. also FBJ Kuiper, 'Some Observations on Dumézil's Theory', in *Numen*, 1961, p. 39; Bernfried Schlerath, *Die Indogermanen: Das Problem der Expansion eines Volkes im Lichte seiner sozialen Struktur* (Innsbruck: Institut für Sprachwissenschaft der Universität, 1973); Jarich G Oosten, *The War of the Gods: The Social Code in Indo-European Mythology* (London: Routledge & Kegan Paul, 1985); Walter W Belier, *Decayed Gods: Origin and Development of Dumézils 'Idéologie Tripartie'* (Leiden: EJ Brill, 1991), and so on. The great majority of these critics, to whom Dumézil never failed to respond, reveal themselves to be futile or irrelevant, and often pivoted on the confusion of their authors.

proach has concealed some significant facts that IE studies should take into account in the future.[352]

Careful to avoid falling back into the 'naturalist' systematisation of a James Frazer or a Max Müller, Dumézil in all likelihood had seriously neglected, by reaction, the cosmic dimension of IE religions and the role that it played in their initial phase. Although as he himself emphasises, 'As important or even central as the ideology of the three functions may be, it is far from constituting the entire Indo-European heritage that comparative analysis can grasp or reconstruct',[353] and here he explicitly dissociates the system of three functions from all systems of universal order, and

---

352 Dumézil, moreover, is deliberately disinterested in certain sectors of the IE domain. He is little concerned with the Anatolian world, with an exception made for the documents of Mitanni. He has above all underestimated the possibility of verifying his theories in the Greek domain, perhaps after having being burnt by some errors committed in the books of his youth. His disciples have been less timid. Cf. especially A Yoshida, 'La structure de l'illustration du bouclier d'Achille', in *Revue belge de philologie et d'histoire*, 1964, pp. 5–15; A Yoshida, 'Survivances de la tripartition fonctionnelle en Grèce', in *Revue de l'histoire des religions*, 1964, pp. 21–38; A Yoshida, 'Le fronton occidental du temple d'Apollon à Delphes et les trois fonctions', in *Revue belge de philologie et d'histoire*, 1966, pp. 5–11; Udo Strutynski, 'The Three Functions of Indo-European Traditions in the "Eumenides" of Aeschylus', in Jaan Puhvel (ed.), *Myth and Law among Indo-Europeans* (Berkeley: University of California Press, 1970), pp. 210–228; C Scott Littleton, 'Some Possible Indo-European Themes in the "Iliad"', ibid., pp. 229–246; R Bodéüs, 'Société athénienne, sagesse grecque et idéal indo-européen', in *L'Antiquité classique*, 1972, pp. 455–486; William T Magrath, 'The Athenian King List and Indo-European Trifunctionality', in *JIES*, Summer 1975, pp. 173–194; Bernard Sergent, 'La représentation spartiate de la royauté', in *Revue de l'histoire des religions*, January 1976, pp. 3–52; Bernard Sergent, 'Les trois fonctions des Indo-Européens dans la Grèce ancienne: bilan critique', in *Annales ESC*, November–December 1979, pp. 1155–1186; Dominique Briquel, 'Initiations grecques et idéologie indo-européenne', in *Annales ESC*, May–June 1982, pp. 454–464; Dominique Briquel, 'Trois recherches sur des traces d'idéologie tripartie en Grèce', in *Etudes indo-européennes*, January 1983, pp. 37–62 & April 1983, pp. 19–33; Jean Haudry, 'Héra', in *Etudes indo-européennes*, September 1983, pp. 17–46 & February 1984, pp. 1–28; Jean Haudry, 'Héra et les héros', in *Etudes indo-européennes*, May 1985, pp. 1–51; Isabelle Leroy-Turcan, 'Persée, vainqueur de la "nuit hivernale" ou le meurtre de Méduse et la naissance des jumeaux solaires Chrysaor et Pégase', in *Etudes indo-européennes*, 1989, pp. 5–17; André Martinet, 'Les Indo-Européens en Grèce', in *Diogène*, January–March 1989, pp. 3–17; and Bernard Sergent, *Les trois fonctions indo-européennes en Grèce ancienne, 1: De Mycènes aux tragiques* (Paris: Economica, 1998).

353 *L'idéologie tripartie des Indo-Européens*, op. cit., p. 189.

never explores either the cosmic character of the general representation of the world among the IE, nor the way in which this representation could have influenced their divisions of time.[354] He worked on the Vedic and Roman dawn, but never attached particular importance to the solar cult, however well attested in Northern Europe, both by the celebrated Solar Chariot discovered at Trundholm and by the rock carvings of Bronze Age Scandinavia. The Sun, along with the diurnal sky, certainly seems to have been the great god of the PIE religion: the traditional formulary preserves no less than five expressions which apply to the Sun or its attributes. The solar cult was probably continued in the cult of fire, notably in the Vedic domain (where Agni is at once an element and a trifunctional god), but also in the Roman and Germanic domains.[355]

Under the expression 'cosmic religion of the Indo-Europeans', Jean Haudry has specifically proposed to gather 'a coherent set of representations by reflecting upon the three principal temporal cycles: the everyday cycle of day, night, sunrise, and sunset; the annual cycle; and the cosmic cycle, each conceived on the model of the daily cycle'.[356] This approach illuminates a more archaic stage of the PIE religion than that characterised by the ideology of three functions, while allowing us to understand how this could have come about. It involves an ancient cosmology of three heavens or skies (diurnal sky, nocturnal sky, and twilight sky; i.e., dawn or dusk) and gives a central importance to certain cosmic entities, with the sunrise taking premier place. It explains the origin of the tripartite

---

354 Cf. Emily V Lyle, 'Dumézil's Three Functions and Indo-European Cosmic Structure', in *History of Religions*, August 1982, pp. 25–44.

355 Cf. Johannes Maringer, 'Fire in Prehistoric Indo-European Europe', in *JIES*, Autumn 1976, pp. 161–186. Marija Gimbutas, for her part, directly connects the funerary rite of cremation with the cult of the Sun and of fire (*The Prehistory of Eastern Europe, 1: Mesolithic, Neolithic and Copper Age Cultures in Russia and the Baltic Area* [Cambridge, MA: Harvard University Press, 1956], p. 82).

356 *La religion cosmique des Indo-Européens* (Milan: Archè & Belles Lettres, 1987), p. 1. Cf. also Jean Haudry, 'Les trois cieux', in *Etudes indo-européennes*, January 1982, pp. 23–48; and 'Les âges du monde, les trois fonctions et la religion cosmique des Indo-Européens', in *Etudes indo-européennes*, 1990, pp. 99–121. The PIE name for 'diurnal sky', *dyew-*, gives rise to both 'sky' and 'day' (and by extension, the word 'god' [*dieu*] < *deywó-*, 'celestial, of the diurnal sky').

ideology by bringing into view among the sovereign divinities of the IE not only the 'luminous' or simply 'celestial' deities, but the representatives of the 'diurnal sky'. It also conducts an analysis of the IE concept of the 'year' as an entity 'with two shores', directly linked to the 'heroic' theme of the 'crossing of the water of wintery darkness': the hero is one who 'conquers the year' by achieving this 'crossing'.[357] In this initial state of the IE religion, the essential theme is the homology of the day and the year ('the year of men is a day of the gods'), and each of these unities was divided into three phases: a descending phase and an ascending phase, with sunrise and sunset interposed between them. Without doubt, this homology justifies taking up the study of the divisions of time among the IE, a domain that has been little studied since Otto Schrader.[358] In our opinion, it has a good chance of being able to demonstrate a year divided into three seasons, along with a division of the lunar months into three periods of eight or nine nights.[359] An in-depth study of the symbolism of the labyrinth and of the double spiral, which seems to be linked to the theme of the Sun's course throughout the year, would also be welcome.[360]

While he did not wish to investigate how the tripartite ideology had been constituted, Dumézil was by no means unaware that the domain he studied had necessarily undergone an evolution. 'Nowhere has he writ-

---

357 For an application of this scheme to Celtic religion, cf. Philippe Jouet, *L'aurore celtique: Fonctions du héros dans la religion cosmique* (Paris: Porte-Glaive, 1994); and 'La structure du panthéon celtique: hypothèses trifonctionnelles et "religion cosmique"', in *Etudes indo-européennes*, 1995, pp. 43–79. On the cosmic religion, but in a completely different context, cf. also Bruce Lincoln, *Myth, Cosmos, and Society: Indo-European Themes of Creation and Destruction* (Cambridge, MA: Harvard University Press, 1986).

358 *Die älteste Zeittheilung des indogermanischen Volkes* (Berlin: Carl Habel, 1878). Cf. also Wolfgang Schultz, *Zeitrechnung und Weltordnung in ihren übereinstimmenden Grundzügen bei den Indern, Iraniern, Hellenen, Italikern, Germanen, Kelten, Litauern, Slawen* (Leipzig: Curt Kabitzsch, 1924).

359 It is interesting to observe that, in all the IE languages, the number 'nine' is homonymous with the adjective 'new' [cf. French *neuf*]. It remains to be seen whether this series of eight or nine nights may also correspond to groups of signs that have divinatory value, which could be the origin of the *Aettir* of the runic script.

360 We ourselves have provided a first draft (in Marc de Smedt, ed., *L'Europe païenne* [Seghers, 1980], pp. 251–364), to which we will return again.

ten, we can be sure, that the historically attested religions resulted from a
simple and linear evolution of the Indo-European religion'.[361] But he had
the tendency to place this evolution below PIE religion, and he preferred
to explain it by subsequent 'deformations' of the primordial pantheon, by
'functional slippage', or by 'gaps' in the tripartite structure of certain IE
systems, which are actually much more likely to be reflections of an archaic state of the religion. This approach projects the ideological or social
model later recognised in the historical IE cultures back onto common,
predialectical IE, without seeking to ask whether this model had itself undergone an evolution from the common stage. The tripartite model thus
becomes a mode of *a priori* mental perception, conscious or unconscious,
but in any event independent of the categories of space and time; the
whole system thus finds itself placed outside the field of historical analysis.

We know today that the system of three functions is primarily an
ideological system, resulting from the cosmic system and which eventually extends itself on the social plane: the ancient IE societies did not all
subdivide into three classes, and, where this was the case, these classes
did not necessarily correspond. But it is still necessary to add that it is by
no means certain that the PIE community had originally known a highly
developed social stratification. It is significant in this regard that the IE
societies which seem to have been the most socially stratified are those
that developed in regions farthest from the homeland, which were conse-
quently in contact with populations that were doubtlessly very different:
at the dawn of our era, the Germanic and Balto-Slavic societies still appeared relatively egalitarian. On the social plane, tripartition also implies
the differentiation of a military caste, which did not necessarily exist in
the original common epoch. Originally, the same individuals probably
exercised a pastoral function in times of peace and a warrior function
when circumstances demanded it, which could explain why gods like
Mars and Thor have, in addition to their warrior character, some distinct
agrarian functions (and also the fact that it is Mars who patronises the

---

361 'L'étude comparée des religions indo-européennes', art. cit., p. 394.

ver sacrum,[362] a religious decree in which the youth are sent off to find a new habitat). When it is indeed attested on the social plane, the 'tripartite' society is born from the fusion of a people consisting uniquely of priest-kings and of warrior-breeders, and a pre-IE people who were given the third function (which, according to Dumézil, is mainly where everything not covered by the framework of the other two takes place). The tripartite system, from this perspective, would correspond to the state of the PIE religion during the stage of its last common habitat (the 'age of heroes'). It is equally during this epoch that the formulas would have been constituted, which researchers (such as Rüdiger Schmitt, Calvert Watkins, Enrico Campanile, and Gregory Nagy) have been able to reconstruct. 'Therefore, in my opinion', write Edgar C Polomé, 'the tripartite ideology is more recent than some of the purely pastoralist traditions that comparative mythology has been retrieving. It originated as the Indo-European community began breaking up — maybe after the departure of the Proto-Anatolians?'[363]

Reticent regarding every 'historicising view',[364] Dumézil has effectively shown that myths could be retranscribed into 'history' (as in Rome), without being willing to admit, however, that historical facts could have given rise to myths.[365] This prudence appears excessive to us. As we have already said, it cannot be ruled out that some IE religious traditions could have conserved the memory of a primordial habitat and of natural catastrophes which accompanied its destruction. Equally, there is good

---

362 The 'sacred spring' was a practice of the ancient Italic peoples, in which young men and women of 20 or 21 years of age would be banished from their homeland as a sacrifice to Mars. — Ed.

363 Cf. Edgar C Polomé, 'Indo-European Culture, with Special Attention to Religion', in EC Polomé (ed.), *The Indo-Europeans in the Fourth and Third Millennia*, op. cit., pp. 162–163.

364 *Les dieux des Germains*, op. cit., p. 16.

365 'The result', writes Alexandre Grandazzi, 'can only be a radical, almost ontological, dissociation between ideas and facts, between an ideology that remained the same throughout all its subsequent metamorphoses and a history condemned to oblivion and nonbeing as a result of that ideology's survival' (*The Foundation of Rome* [Ithaca: Cornell University Press, 1997], p. 44).

reason to think that the IE myths of 'wars of foundation'—corresponding to the war between the Ases (*Æsir*) and the Vanes (*Vanir*) among the
Germanic peoples, the war of the Sabines among the Romans, the epic
of the *Mahabharata* among the Indians, perhaps also the *Iliad* among
the Greeks, and certain passages of the *Lebor Gabala Erenn* and of the
Mabinogi among the Celts — do not merely constitute a narrative seeking
to produce, in a dramatic form, an 'ideological' lesson about the functioning rules of a community and the hierarchy of functions it assumes. It may
also refer to an actually occurring 'cultural' conflict, whether internal to
the PIE community, or between the original IE people (representing the
two primary functions) and a pre-IE population (representing the third)
upon which the first two functions are superimposed, thus indicating
the manner in which the conflict was settled. Such a hypothesis cannot
be rejected since we know that most of the historic IE societies were in
fact born from the confrontation, and then fusion, of two different kinds
of people (and therefore two sociocultural and symbolic systems). Thus,
André Martinet evokes 'the opposition of Ases and Vanes, where the first
could represent the pantheon of newcomers, and the second the ancient
chthonic and indigenous divinities'.[366] This is also the opinion of Edgar C
Polomé, who writes, 'The Indo-Europeans, in the course of their migrations and of their expansion, are constantly entering into contact with
sedentary, agricultural populations, upon which they impose themselves
and which are "absorbed" into their social structure, a symbiosis that must
have created from the beginning the kinds of tensions between heteroge-
neous and often antithetical orientations that Georges Dumézil described
in his commentaries by the war of the Sabines and the parallel conflict
opposing the *Æsir* and *Vanir* in Scandinavian mythology'.[367]

---

366 'Les Indo-Européens et la Grèce', art. cit., p. 15.

367 'Indo-European Culture, with Special Attention to Religion', art. cit., pp. 164–165. We
     know that the 'Odhinic' kingship was only imposed very slowly in the Scandinavian
     countries, and that the 'Vanic' kingship perpetuates itself from the seventh century
     CE. Cf. Jean-Paul Allard, 'La royauté wotanique des Germains, I', in *Etudes indo-
     européennes*, January 1982, pp. 76–77.

2. Indo-European Languages and Pre-Indo-European Languages

There has been much speculation about the idea of a 'pre-IE substrate'. This notion corresponds to an undeniable reality, which, we have seen, is not always easily discernible. For Marija Gimbutas, this substrate is principally represented by the cultures of 'Old Europe', that is, by the great urban, agricultural civilisations that were covered over or destroyed by the IE expansion. The problem is that we know virtually nothing about the language or languages which these cultures used. In many respects, the notion of the 'pre-IE substrate' is a kind of catchall in which we have previously placed the Pelasgians, the Etruscans, cultures derived from the Palaeolithic, and cultures from the Megalithic, as well as Mediterranean populations called, for better or worse, 'Asiatic', and so on.

In a certain number of cases, it cannot be ruled out that what we once considered a 'pre-IE substrate' will turn out in reality to be a previously unidentified IE substrate. The fact that the IE character of Anatolian languages such as Hittite, Luwian, Lycian (a late form of Luwian), and Lydian (a late form of Hittite) has only been recognised relatively late, has motivated us to re-examine the case of a certain number of other languages. We know today that the arrival of the IE in Anatolia presents itself less as an invasion and more as a slow process of infiltration.[368] Researchers now ask whether some Aegean languages, or languages from Asia Minor that Paul Kretschmer[369] qualified in the nineteenth century as 'Asiatic', such as Carian, Pamphylian, Pisidian, Cydonian, Eteocretan, and so on, might also be IE languages. According to Emil Forrer and Leonard R Palmer, many IE languages preceding Greek in the Aegean basin are derived from Luwian. Other scholars, after Eric Hamp, connect them to the northwest group.

---

368 Cf. Friedrich Cornelius, *Geschichte der Hethiter*, op. cit., pp. 43–45 & 292–293.

369 *Einleitung in die Geschichte der griechischen Sprache* (Göttingen: Vandenhoeck & Ruprecht, 1896).

We know that, even in the historical epoch, many different languages were still spoken in Greece.[370] For a long time we have brought the speakers of these languages, believed to be developed in the Greek peninsula before the arrival of the Greeks, under the convenient label 'Pelasgic': a population to which we attribute an 'Aegean' or vaguely specified 'Mediterranean' origin. The dominant opinion today is that the Pelasgians were indeed IE, but not Greek. In the name of their mythic ancestor, Teutamos, given by Homer in the *Odyssey*, we recognise the root *teuta-*, attested in Illyrian, Osco-Umbrian, Celtic, Germanic, and Baltic, with the sense of 'people, community', which we rediscover in the name of the Gallic god Toutatis, or in that of the 'Teutons'. Philip M Freeman[371] has shown that before the arrival of the Greeks in the peninsula, some languages spoken by their predecessors already included the labiovelars (*qa, qe, qi*), which suggests that their speakers were IE populations which had penetrated into Greece earlier (from Anatolia according to Freeman). Michel B Sakellariou[372] sees the Pelasgians as the principle IE component of the pre-Hellenic population of Greece, alongside the Dryopes and Haimones, but has them come from Northern Europe at a date prior to the formation of the Kurgans. After Budimir, the original form of their ethnic name would be *Pelast-, Pelaist-*. In this, Sakellariou sees the name of an ancient vegetation god, derived from IE *bhel-* 'bloom, sprout, swell'. The Pelasgians (*Pelastoi*) could have been the ancestors of the Philistines (Hebrew *Pelisht-im, Pulashati; prsht* in Egyptian documents), who participated with the 'Sea Peoples from the North' in the attack against the Egyptian empire of Ramses III. Basing themselves on the similarity of Greek and Anatolian toponyms, some authors think that the Pelasgic language belongs to Luwian. Others, prob-

---

370   Cf. Homer, *Odyssey*: 'Out in the wine-dark sea lies a land called Crete, a rich and fair land begirt with water. It is filled with countless people, in ninety cities. They are not of one language, but speak several tongues. There are Achaeans there, and great-hearted Eteocretans, Cydonians, Dorians in three clans, and noble Pelasgians' (XIX, 175 ff.).

371   'New Evidence for Pre-Greek Labiovelars', in *JIES*, Spring–Summer 1989, pp. 171–176. Cf. also F Kuiper, 'Pre-Hellenic Labio-Velars', in *Lingua*, 1968, pp. 269–277.

372   *Peuples préhelléniques d'origine indo-européenne* (Athens: Ekdotikè Athenon, 1977).

ably more justly, opt for another, unidentified IE language, perhaps related to Thracian. Vladimir Georgiev thinks that this language has undergone a consonantal mutation comparable to that of Germanic or Armenian. He also shows that the characteristic suffixes in '-nth-', '-inthos', '-ss' (which we find in names like 'Corinth', 'Tyrinth', 'hyacinth', 'labyrinth', 'jacinthe', etc.), long considered as non-IE because non-Greek, are also of IE origin.

Fred C Woudhuizen[373] believes that the inscriptions on the famous Phaistos Disk[374] are notes in Luwian. For Edgar Bowden,[375] it is a Greek text with Luwian loans. Eteocretan, recorded in Linear A, is also interpreted by Georgiev as an ancient form of Luwian. Paul Faure,[376] for whom Linear A (which he believes to be more recent than Linear B) already contains the dative plural in '-si-', the instrumental, and athematic conjugations, also asserts that the builders of the Cretan 'palace' of Zakro in Cydonia spoke an IE language.

We have also long considered Etruscan to be a non-IE language, akin for some to the pre-IE languages of Western Europe, and for others to the pre-IE languages of Asia Minor. From 1939, Paul Kretschmer[377] has maintained that it was from a 'Proto-IE' language, close to the Pelasgian speakers on the Greek peninsula, who were separated very early from common IE and first developed in Lydia. From 1943, Vladimir Georgiev[378] saw it as a 'western' form of Lydian, that is, of Late Hittite. More recently,

373 *The Language of the Sea Peoples* (Amsterdam: Najade Press, 1992).

374 The Phaistos Disk, which has been dated to the second millennium BCE, was discovered in 1908 on Crete. Its inscriptions have yet to be decoded. — Ed.

375 *Cybele, the Axe Goddess: Alliterative Verse, Linear B Relationships and Cult Ritual of the Phaistos Disk* (Amsterdam: Gieben, 1992).

376 'Du caractère indo-européen de la langue écrite en Crète à l'âge du bronze moyen', in *Etudes indo-européennes*, March 1984, pp. 1–23; and 'Onomastique crétoise préhellénique', in *Etudes indo-européennes*, 1987, pp. 65–79.

377 'Die Stellung der lykischen Sprache', in *Glotta*, 1939, 27, pp. 256–267, & 28, pp. 101–116.

378 *Die sprachliche Zugehörigkeit des Etruskischen*, Sofia 1943; 'Etruskisch ist Späthethitisch', in *Die Sprache*, 1964, pp. 169–167; 'Etruskisch und Hethitisch: Ein Vergleich der bekannten Tatsachen der etruskischen Grammatik', in *Linguistique balkanique*, 1974, pp. 5–40.

Francisco Rodriguez Adrados[379] has defended the thesis that Etruscan is a very archaic IE language, close in its phonetics and morphology to the IE languages of Anatolia, but even more ancient than these: it would be a proto-Anatolian language, formed at the very beginning of the appearance of inflection in common IE. For his part, Fred C Wouldhuizen assimilates Etruscan to Luwian.[380] In 1976, James Wellard listed twelve Caucasian languages which could be related to Etruscan. A connection with Hurrian has also been attempted. Siding with the opinion of Herodotus,[381] according to whom the Etruscans were originally from Lydia, which confirms the 'orientalising' character of their art (as well as the absence of all archaeological traces of their presence in Mesolithic Italy), Georgiev sees them as the descendants of the Trojans, whose name reflects that of the city of Troy (*Troses* > *E-trus-ci*). The (E)truscans, then known under the name of *Tursha*, also participated in the assault by the 'Sea Peoples from the North' against the Egyptian empire in the thirteenth century BCE, installing themselves in northern Italy after their defeat. The Roman legend of Aeneas and Anchises preserves the memory of their former homeland. This hypothesis would also explain the similarity of the Etruscan cremation urns to some Caucasian houses and Cretan tombs. While the thesis of a language at once autochthonous and non-IE retains its adherents, notably among Italian linguists,[382] the other points of view are increasingly starting to prevail today. Etruscan is included as a 'peri-Indo-European' language in a recent book on the IE languages edited by Françoise Bader.[383]

---

379 'Etruscan as an Indo-European Anatolian (but Not Hittite) Language', in *JIES*, Autumn–Winter 1989, pp. 363–383.

380 'Etruscan and Luwian', in *JIES*, 1991, pp. 133–150. Cf. also Edgar Bowden, 'Caucasus-Aegean-Etruria: A Bronze Age Etrusco-Luwian Diffusion', in *The Mankind Quarterly*, Winter 1994–95, pp. 209–318.

381 Herodotus (c. 484–425 BCE) was a Greek historian who is regarded as the first to treat history in a critical way rather than as myth. — Ed.

382 Cf. Giuliano & L Bonfante, *The Etruscan Language: An Introduction* (Manchester: Manchester University Press, 2002).

383 *Langues indo-européennes*, op. cit., pp. 319–330.

Considered by Marija Gimbutas as 'still living Old Europeans', the Basques seem to constitute the only European population that survived at least four thousand years worth of invasions. In any case, their language is the only pre-IE language still spoken today in Europe. (We only possess written evidence for Iberian). The researchers who have weighed in on their case are divided between those who, basing themselves above all on the physical form of the Basque population, think that they already occupied their current territory in the Upper Palaeolithic, and those who see them as the descendants of a pre-IE Central European population which would have been repelled westward by the IE invasions, where they would have then mixed with an autochthonous Iberian element. The hypothesis has also been advanced that Basque would have been the final representative of a pre-IE language which was previously distributed across all of Europe. We have thus assimilated Basque *adar*, 'corn', with Old-Irish *adarc*, with the same meaning, a word for which there is no known IE etymology: the two terms could come from the same substrate. We have also compared the Basque words *mutur*, 'face', and *doino*, 'popular song', and the Romanian words *mutra* and *doina*, with the same meaning. More recently, Theo Vennemann[384] has connected some Basque words with hydronyms which are attested in the IE languages but which do not seem to come from PIE. Other convergences, generally unfruitful, have been attempted with Minoan, Etruscan, Sumerian, Pictish, and Berber. The most frequently held hypothesis, notably by Christian C Uhlenbeck,[385] Alfredo Trombetti,[386] Karl Bouda,[387] Georges Dumézil,[388] and René Lafon,[389] is

---

384 'Linguistic Reconstruction in the Context of European Prehistory', in *Transactions of the Philological Society*, 1994, pp. 215–284.

385 'De la possibilité d'une parenté entre le basque et les langues caucasiques', in *Revista internacional de los estudios vascos*, 1924, pp. 564–588.

386 *Origini della lingua basca* (Bologna: A Forni, 1925).

387 *Baskisch-Kaukasische Etymologien* (Heidelberg: Carl Winter, 1949).

388 *Introduction à la grammaire comparée des langues caucasiennes du Nord* (Paris: H Champion, Bibliothèque de l'Institut français de Léningrad, 1933), pp. 123–149.

389 'La linguistique basque et caucasique', in *Revue de l'enseignement supérieur*, 1967, pp. 56–66.

that of a kinship between Basque and certain non-IE languages of the north Caucasus. This thesis, which is based on a certain number of typological and above all terminological resemblances, nevertheless remains contested[390] despite evidence of certain genetic similarities.[391] In fact no solution allows us at the present time to connect the Basque language, in an incontestable manner, to any other language, living or dead.[392]

The apparent absence in the Basque language of any borrowings from the IE system of languages also remains unexplained. It seems to testify *a priori* to a great isolation of the Basque populations since very remote times. However, we also do not find any loans from the Germanic languages, even though the Basques had been in contact with the Visigoths and Franks for many centuries. Antonio Tovar[393] has attempted to demonstrate that the use of the Basque suffix '-*ko*' is sufficiently close to the PIE suffix '*-*ko*' (attested in all IE languages, save Hittite) in order to derive them both from a common stem, but this opinion is also not unanimous.

3. The Origins of Writing

'The Neolithic peoples of Eastern Europe did not write', affirms Bernard Sergent.[394] The idea that writing would appear in Europe under the influence of the Near East via the intermediary of scripts gradually derived from the Sumerian pictographic system, and more specifically from the Phoenician script, which developed itself in Crete from the eleventh century BCE and which would give birth to the Greek and Latin alphabets, can no longer be sustained today. Thanks to radiocarbon dating, we now actually know that a script was already used at the beginning of

---

390 Cf. Luis Michelena, *Sobre historia de la lengua vasca*, 2 vols. (Donostia-San Sebastián: Diputación de Gipuzkoa, 1988).

391 Cf. Luyca L Cavalli-Sforza et al., *The History and Geography of Human Genes*, op. cit.

392 Cf. RL Traks, 'Origin and Relatives of the Basque Language: Review of the Evidence', in José Ignacio Hualde, Joseba A Lakarra, & RL Traks (eds.), *Towards a History of the Basque Language* (Amsterdam: John Benjamins, 1995), pp. 65–99.

393 'El suffijo "-ko": indoeuropeo y circumindoeuropeo', in *Archivio glottologico italiano*, 1954, pp. 56–64.

394 *Les Indo-Européens*, op. cit., p. 386.

the Neolithic in the Danube Valley, close to Belgrade, in the cultures of 'Old Europe' from Vinča and Karanovo. This script, which is much older than the Sumerian pictographs (which do not appear until the end of the fourth millennium), was used from the end of the sixth millennium until around 3500 BCE; that is, until the arrival of the IE in the region. It has been studied by MA Georgievskij since 1940. Contrary to the writing systems of the ancient Near East (Egyptian hieroglyphics, Hittite and Luwian hieroglyphics, Sumerian cuneiform), this script is of a linear and seemingly logographic type (where each sign expresses a concept), not phonographic (where each sign equates to an individual sound or syllable). It draws on a reduced number of signs: 220 in total, with variations for 36 of them. The inscriptions discovered to this day, in more than thirty different sites, are generally brief, and only figure on objects of a ritual or votive character. This script has obviously not been deciphered, and its decipherment seems to be unlikely, since we do not know any of the languages spoken in this region before the arrival of the IE.[395]

With the arrival of the IE, the Danubian cultures of 'Old Europe' were driven towards the Aegean, Crete, and the Cyclades. HG Buchholz[396] suggested that their script could have been the origin of Cretan Linear A. This latter script, which seems to include both ideograms and phonograms, was the most widespread Cretan writing system: we find it on Cyprus, on most of the islands of the Aegean Sea, through to the Aeolian Islands north of Sicily. It is from these that the other scripts are formed, like the Cypro-Minoan syllabary (from the sixteenth century BCE), Linear B (from the fifteenth), and the Cypriot syllabary (from the eleventh). It cannot be ruled

---

395 Cf. MM Winn, *The Signs of Vinca Culture*, Dissertation, University of California, 1973; MM Winn, *Pre-Writing in Southern Europe: The Sign System of the Vinca Culture, ca. 4000 BC*, Alberta 1981; and Emilia Masson, 'L'écriture dans les civilisations danubiennes néolithiques', in *Kadmos*, 1984, pp. 89–123. Cf. also Hans Jensen, *Sign, Symbol and Script: An Account of Man's Efforts to Write* (New York: Putnam, 1969); and K Földes-Papp, *Vom Felsbild zum Alphabet: Die Geschichte der Schrift von ihren frühesten Vorstufen bis zur modernen lateinischen Schreibschrift* (Bayreuth: Gondrom, 1975 & Stuttgart-Zürich: Belser, 1987).

396 'Die ägäischen Schriftsysteme und ihre Ausstrahlung in die ostmediterranen Kulturen', in *Frühe Schriftzeugnisse der Menschheit*, Göttingen 1969, pp. 88–150.

out that it also played a role in the appearance of the Syro-Palestinian alphabetic script. On the basis of many similarities with the Danubian script (around a third of the signs are the same), Harald Harrmann[397] believes that it had formed, together with Cretan hieroglyphic, the script of a priest caste. Parallel to this, some signs have taken an independent symbolic value in Crete, such as the spiral and the double-headed axe, of which we already find stylised forms in the writings from Vinča, whereas others, like the swastika, subsisted primarily as decorative elements.

Other similarities have been raised with the pre-IE script of the Indus Valley. This script has been known for a long time: more than 4,200 objects bearing inscriptions of various lengths have been uncovered at different sites belonging to the Harappa and Mohenjo-Daro cultures. The number of signs used was 401.[398] This script also does not derive from the writing systems of the Near East. Subhash C Kak[399] believes that it influenced the first Sanskrit inscriptions, but this hypothesis remains to be demonstrated.

This data might one day shed new light on the numerous researches which have been done into the symbolism of rock carvings, as well as the signs and series of signs that appear in the Upper Palaeolithic which we generally class under the denomination 'pre-writings'.[400] From Aurignacian, such signs have served to record the subdivisions of lunar 'phrasing' over a period of many months, thanks to incisions made into

---

397 'Writing from Old Europe to Ancient Crete: A Case of Cultural Continuity', in *JIES*, Autumn–Winter 1989, pp. 251–275.

398 Cf. GR Hunter, *The Script of Harappa and Mohenjodaro and its Connection with Other Scripts* (London: Kegan Paul Trench Trubner & Co., 1934); ASC Ross, *The Numeral-Signs of the Mohenjo-Daro Script* (New Delhi: Archaeological Survey of India, 1938); I Mahadevan, *The Indus Scripts: Texts, Concordance and Tables* (New Delhi: Archaeological Survey of India, 1977); JE Mitchiner, *Studies in the Indus Valley Inscriptions* (New Delhi: Oxford, 1978); and Asko Parpola, *Deciphering the Indus Script* (New York: Cambridge University Press, 1994).

399 'On the Decipherment of the Indus Script: A Preliminary Study of its Connection with Brahmi', in *Indian Journal of History of Science*, 1987, pp. 51–62; and 'Indus Writing', in *The Mankind Quarterly*, Autumn–Winter 1989, pp. 113–118.

400 Cf. Mathieu Maxime Gorce, *Les pré-écritures et l'évolution des civilisations, 18 000 à 8000 ans avant J.-C.* (Paris: Klincsieck, 1974).

stone, bone, and without doubt also wood (the most ancient IE root for 'write', *peyk-, originally meant 'to cut, engrave').[401] We find it again in the Salzmünde group of the Funnel Beaker culture. It seems reasonable to think that, from the remotest of times, a certain number of logographic signs have been used for purposes of symbolic representation or for religious ends, in particular divination, in connection with the discovery of temporal divisions, and then developing towards actual systems of pictographic or phonographic writing. Such has necessarily been the case, at least with a certain number of signs, with the runic 'alphabet' (futhark). Although not attested before the second century BCE (the dating of the inscription of the Negau helmet[402] discovered in Yugoslavia remains disputed), this script, by reason of its structural peculiarities (different letter order, grouping of signs in three rows of eight or aettir, letters lacking equivalents, a proper name and value attributed to each letter), cannot be explained, in our opinion, only as a local derivation of an Etruscan or north Italic alphabet. It more likely results from an adaptation to an alphabetic system of a set of signs previously used for divinatory or 'cosmological' ends, as testified by the fact that the god Odhinn-Wotan is regularly described as the 'master of the runes'.

---

401 'It seems', writes Alexander Marshack, 'in an epoch as remote as 30,000 years BCE, during the glacial period, that the Western European hunter had made use of a complex, previously evolved system of notation, whose tradition could reach back several thousand years. Apparently, other types of modern humans also used it, such as the Combe-Capelle man and that of the Eastern Gravettian culture in Czechoslovakia and Russia. [...] [These notations] do not yet represent a script in the sense that we understand it. Nevertheless, it seems that we can see the roots of science and writing, to the degree that we have archaeological evidence that indicates, according to all appearances, the existence within this man of the same basic *cognitive processes* that will appear later in science and in writing'. (*The Roots of Civilization* [New York: McGraw-Hill Book Co., 1970); French ed.: *Les racines de la civilisation: Les sources cognitives de l'art, du symbole et de la notation chez les premiers hommes* (Paris: Plon, 1972, pp. 57-58). Cf. also Alexander Marshack, 'On Paleolithic Ochre and the Early Uses of Color and Symbol', in *Current Anthropology*, April 1981, pp. 188-191; and Hal Porter, 'A Startling Look at Ice Age Innovators', in *Science Digest*, December 1982, pp. 69-72.

402 The Negau helmet is an Etruscan artifact that was discovered in Slovenia in 1812, dating to about 50 BCE. Scholars continue to argue about the meaning and significance of the inscription on it. — Ed.

4. From PIE to 'Nostratic'

In the 1960s, two Russian linguists, Vladislav Illich-Svitych and Aron Dolgopolsky, independently developed a theory postulating the existence, at a very remote date, of a language family called 'Nostratic'. It allegedly forms the common stem of not only the PIE languages, but also the Kartvelian (Caucasian), Uralic, Dravidian, Altaic, and Hamito-Semitic languages. From certain supposed resemblances between Basque, the languages of the Caucasus, the Sino-Tibetan languages, Na-Dene, Burushaski, and so on, other authors have imagined a 'Eurasian' linguistic family, whose presence in Western Europe corresponds to the arrival of modern humans, some 40,000 years ago. The affinities between the Semitic languages and the Finno-Ugric languages were already noted in the eighteenth century by the Spanish Jesuit Lorenzo Hervas. Gamkrelidze and Ivanov believe, for their part, that a number of PIE words are Proto-Semitic loans, and that a number of Proto-Kartvelian words are borrowings from PIE. It goes without saying that all these theories, by reason of the fragility of the data upon which they are based, remain largely speculative.

Numerous attempts have been made since the beginning of the twentieth century to connect PIE and Proto-Semitic.[403] They bring up some morphological similarities, especially in the consonantism and prenominal system, but the demonstration as a whole remains largely unconvinc-

---

403 Cf. Hermann Møller, *Semitisch und Indogermanisch, 1: Konsonanten* (København: H Hagerup, 1906) (reprint: Hildesheim: Georg Olms, 1978); Hermann Møller, *Indoeuropaeisk-semitisk sammenlignende glossarium* (København: H Hagerup, 1909; German ed.: *Vergleichendes indogermanische-semitisches Wörterbuch* [Göttingen: Vandenhoeck & Ruprecht, 1911); Albert Cuny, *Etudes prégrammaticales sur le domaine des langues indo-européennes et chamito-sémitiques*, (Paris: Edouard Champion, 1924); Albert Cuny, *La catégorie du duel dans les langues indo-européennes et chamito-sémitiques* (Brussels: Havez, 1930; Albert Cuny, *Recherches sur le vocalisme, le consonantisme et la formation des racines en 'nostratique', ancêtre de l'indo-européen et du chamito-sémitique* (Paris: Adrien Maisonneuve, 1943); Linus Brunner, *Die gemeinsamen Wurzeln des semitischen und indogermanischen Wortschatzes: Versuch einer Etymologie* (Bern-Munich: Francke, 1969); and Saul Levin, *The Indo-European and Semitic Languages: An Exploration of Structural Similarities Related to Accent, Chiefly in Greek, Sanskrit, and Hebrew* (Albany, NY: State University of New York Press, 1971).

ing. The phonological system in particular is completely different. The vowel system is richer in the IE languages. Lexical similarities only reach around 150 words.[404] If the two language families are related, they were separated at a very early date.[405] M Kaiser and V Shevoroshkin[406] have furthermore shown that the majority of loans assumed by Gamkrelidze and Ivanov must be rejected for reasons both semantic and phonetic.[407]

The only group of non-IE languages presenting some affinities with PIE is the Uralic family of languages, of which the Finno-Ugric languages (Finnish, Estonian, Hungarian, Lappic) represent the western branch, while the Samoyed languages of the north and Siberia represent the eastern branch. The affinities are especially strong with the Finno-Ugric languages, and, within those, their western branch, principally represented by Finnish. Analysis of the phonetic structure and the diffusion of loans shows that they date back to an era preceding the first IE migrations, at least to the beginning of the fifth millennium, at a time when the Finnish and Ugrian group (notably represented by Hungarian) were already separated.[408] From the third millennium, the Finno-Ugrians also

---

404 We have, for example, connected the IE name for 'bull' [French *taureau*], *tauros* (Greek *tauros*, Lithuanian *taûras*), to Phonecian *thor*, Ugaritic *thr*, Syrian *twar*. But comparisons of this order, which are isolated occurences, rarely have demonstrative value.

405 Cf. Allan R Bomhard, 'The I.E.-Semitic Hypothesis Re-Examined', in *JIES*, Spring 1977, pp. 55–99.

406 'Inheritance versus Borrowing in Indo-European, Kartvelian, and Semitic', in *JIES*, Autumn–Winter 1986, pp. 365–378.

407 Contrary to what Gamkrelidze and Ivanov assert, who see it as a loan from the Semitic languages, there is indeed a PIE name for 'star', *Hs-tér* (cf. Hittite *haster*, Sanskrit *tara*, Tokcharian B *scirye*, Greek *astno*, Latin *stella*, Gothic *stairno*, Old High German *sterno*, Old Norse *stjarna*, Cornish *sterenn*, German *Stern*, French *étoille*, English *star*), derived from a root *as-*, 'to burn, to glow [red]'. Cf. Allan R Bombard, 'An Etymological Note: PIE "*Hs-tér-", "Star"', in *JIES*, Spring–Summer 1986.

408 Cf. Harald Haarmann, 'Contact Linguistics, Archaeology and Ethnogenetics: An Interdisciplinary Approach to the Indo-European Homeland Problem', art. cit., pp. 279–280.

made numerous borrowings from the Indo-Iranian group,[409] which tends to confirm the archaeological data concerning the material culture of the Volga-Samara-Don zone. Finnish *porsas*, 'pig', for example, represents an obvious borrowing from Indo-Iranian *parsa, not from IE *porco-. These two levels of relations and loans are not mutually exclusive. The striking similarities that we can raise between PIE and Proto-Uralic, especially those concerning the personal endings of the verb system and some case endings of names, suggest that the Uralic populations and the PIE had lived in each others' vicinity, and that they shared some sites. The original homeland of the Finno-Ugrians is fairly well identified. It is situated over a territory spanning from the northeast of the Baltic across Russia, to the west of the Urals. This homeland could have been contiguous with that of the PIE. More remotely, it cannot be excluded that PIE and Proto-Uralian were differentiated from a single stem, Proto-Indo-Uralic. The similarities between PIE and the Uralo-Altaic languages have led some Russian researchers to postulate the existence of a 'Boreal linguistic group'.

The convergence with Kartvelian, in other words the principal linguistic group represented in the south Caucasus, seems to show typological similarities in the phonetic and grammatical systems. The proposition of Illich Svitych to connect Kartvelian to PIE in the context of the 'Nostratic' hypothesis was the subject of a debate between Georgij A Klimov and Alexis Manaster Ramer.[410] The question remains open.

---

409 Cf. Björn Collinder, *Finno-Ugric Vocabulary: An Etymological Dictionary of the Uralic Languages* (Stockholm, 1955; 2nd ed.: Hamburg 1977).

410 Georgij A Klimov, 'Some Thoughts on Indo-European-Kartvelian Relations', in *JIES*, 1991, pp. 325–341; and Alexis Manaster Ramer, 'On "Some Thoughts on Indo-European-Kartvelian Relations"', in *JIES*, Spring–Summer 1995, pp. 195–208.

INDEX

OTHER BOOKS PUBLISHED BY ARKTOS

OTHER BOOKS PUBLISHED BY ARKTOS

DANIEL S. FORREST   *Suprahumanism*

ANDREW FRASER   *The WASP Question*

DANIEL FRIBERG   *The Real Right Returns*

GÉNÉRATION IDENTITAIRE   *We are Generation Identity*

PAUL GOTTFRIED   *War and Democracy*

PORUS HOMI HAVEWALA   *The Saga of the Aryan Race*

RACHEL HAYWIRE   *The New Reaction*

LARS HOLGER HOLM   *Hiding in Broad Daylight*
                                     Homo Maximus
                                     Incidents of Travel in Latin America
                                     The Owls of Afrasiab

ALEXANDER JACOB   *De Naturae Natura*

JASON REZA JORJANI   *Prometheus and Atlas*

RODERICK KAINE   *Smart and SeXy*

PETER KING   *Here and Now*
                                     *Keeping Things Close: Essays on
                                     the Conservative Disposition*

LUDWIG KLAGES   *The Biocentric Worldview*
                                     *Cosmogonic Reflections: Selected
                                     Aphorisms from Ludwig Klages*

OTHER BOOKS PUBLISHED BY ARKTOS

Management Mantras

Patanjali Yoga Sutras

Secrets of Relationships

TROY SOUTHGATE

Tradition & Revolution

OSWALD SPENGLER

Man and Technics

TOMISLAV SUNIC

Against Democracy and Equality

ABIR TAHA

Defining Terrorism: The End of Double Standards

The Epic of Arya (Second edition)

Nietzsche's Coming God, or the Redemption of the Divine

Verses of Light

BAL GANGADHAR TILAK

The Arctic Home in the Vedas

DOMINIQUE VENNER

The Shock of History

MARKUS WILLINGER

A Europe of Nations

Generation Identity

DAVID J. WINGFIELD (ED.)

The Initiate: Journal of Traditional Studies

CPSIA information can be obtained
at www.ICGtesting.com
Printed in the USA
LVOW07s1008280617
539640LV00001B/239/P